The Valuation Businesses and Shares:
A Practitioner's Perspective

The Valuation of Businesses and Shares:
A Practitioner's Perspective

Des Peelo

Chartered Accountants Ireland

Published by
Chartered Accountants Ireland
Chartered Accountants House
47-49 Pearse Street
Dublin 2
www.charteredaccountants.ie

© The Institute of Chartered Accountants in Ireland 2010

Copyright of publication rests in entirety with The Institute of Chartered Accountants in Ireland. All rights reserved. No part of this text may be reproduced or transmitted in any form or by any means, including photocopying, Internet or e-mail dissemination, without the written permission of The Institute of Chartered Accountants in Ireland. Such written permission must also be obtained before any part of this document is stored in a retrieval system of any nature.

This publication is designed to provide accurate and authoritative information in regard to the subject matter covered. It is provided on the understanding that The Institute of Chartered Accountants in Ireland is not engaged in rendering professional services. If professional advice or other expert assistance is required, the services of a competent professional should be sought.

No responsibility for loss occasioned to any person as a result of any material in this publication will be accepted by the author or publisher. Readers are advised to take appropriate legal and tax advice in relation to all matters herein. The case histories are not identifiable to any particular situations and are composites of similar circumstances.

ISBN 978-1-907214-30-1

Typeset by Amnet
Printed by ColourBooks

Contents

Chapter 1 The Role of the Valuer 1
'Benign' and 'angry' valuations – valuer's duties and responsibilities – Letter of Engagement – the auditor as valuer

Chapter 2 The Fundamentals of Valuation 10
The right to receive future income is being valued – Rules of Thumb – the size of shareholding and voting influence – the role of net assets

Chapter 3 Future Maintainable Profits 29
Simple average and weighted average – business risk is on three levels – no certainty in business forecasts – pricing power – balance sheet analysis

Chapter 4 The Multiple 39
Historic P/Es in Ireland – hindsight has no part – UK indices – Revenue guidelines – suggested multiples

Chapter 5 The Minority Position 54
Practice and Revenue guidelines on discount – dividend valuation – 'embarrassment clause' – no new thinking on minority valuations

Chapter 6 The Role of Assets 59
'Unit valuation principle' – definition of net assets – age of assets and replacement – property and investment companies – goodwill

Chapter 7 Rules of Thumb 69
Irrational approach – 'formula purchases' – pubs and hotels – preliminary indication as to a seller's expectation of price

Chapter 8 Grievance is not a Method of Valuation 73
Client expectations – difficulties regarding obtaining information – 'Letter of Confidentiality'

Chapter 9 Valuing a Small Business 78

No active market – transition process in sale – third-party complications

Chapter 10 Discounted Cash Flows (DCF) 81

Difficulties of estimating future profits – the discount rate – drawbacks of DCF

Chapter 11 A Quasi-partnership 85

Case law rather than statutory law – tests as to existence – effect on valuation of a minority shareholding

Chapter 12 The Special Purchaser 89

Definition – relevance to valuation – paying for own opportunity and / or expertise

Chapter 13 A Shareholders' Agreement 92

The five key provisions – deadlock and 'Russian Roulette'

Chapter 14 Fair Value, Market Value and Willing Buyer / Willing Seller 96

Definitions – focus is on what a purchaser is willing to pay – interpretations for tax purposes

Chapter 15 A Management Buyout 101

No difference in approach to valuation

Chapter 16 Intellectual Property 105

Insufficient market transactions to establish valuation guidelines

Chapter 17 A Professional Practice 108

There is no 'norm' on valuation – role of Partnership Act 1890 – dissolution – goodwill

Appendix One Example of Letter of Confirmation from Directors 129

Appendix Two Examples of Letters of Engagement: 133

    A: A straightforward valuation in non-contested circumstances 139
    B: A valuation in contested circumstances 143
    C: An indicative 'desktop' valuation 149
    D: An informal explanation / analysis of a modest business 151

Appendix Three Examples of Valuation Reports: 153

    A: A straightforward valuation in non-contested circumstances 155
    B: A valuation in contested circumstances 159
    C: An indicative 'desktop' valuation 163

Appendix Four Revenue Guidelines on Share Valuation 165

Appendix Five The Partnership Act 1890 177

Appendix Six Tables of Present Value 199

Index 203

Foreword

This book is intended to be read and used in a practical way. The intention is that the practitioner, having made due enquiry as suggested, can then prepare a valuation suitable for purpose. Most of all, the book provides the words and explanations that are necessary for the practitioner in communicating with the end user (be that an individual, the directors of a company, a financial institution, or as an expert witness in court) as to what the valuation is and as to what it is not. (Experienced practitioners will already know why there is a chapter entitled "Grievance is not a Method of Valuation" (Chapter 8).)

The opening chapters of the book, Chapters 1 and 2, work together. Starting with the duties and responsibilities of the valuer, the book then sets out the fundamentals, or perhaps more correctly, *the rules*, to be followed in carrying out a valuation.

The familiar characteristics of valuation then follow in individual chapters: future maintainable profits (Chapter 3), the multiple, or P/E ratio (Chapter 4), and the role of assets (Chapter 6). The vexed question of the minority position is considered separately in Chapter 5. There is a short chapter on *'Rules of Thumb'* (Chapter 7) sometimes the bane of a valuer in trying to address the often-held belief that a valuation is really just a question of following a *'pre-ordained formula'* or *'norm'* of some kind.

The instructions for most valuations probably start in the legal world, often arising through a dispute, an estate or the sale of a shareholding or business. While this is not a legal text, the practitioner will notice the legal involvement in many of the valuation aspects referred to in this book. At the same time, the legal world likes certainty and precedent, which is not always possible or available in valuation. For example, a practitioner will often have to grapple with what is meant by *'Fair value, market value and willing buyer/willing seller'* (as set out in the Articles of a company or in a legal agreement), and there is a chapter here on that subject (Chapter 14).

The practitioner will likely welcome the chapter on "Valuing a Small Business" (Chapter 9), the difficulty here being as to whether the business has a value at all and then trying to explain this to a client who wants to sell it or retire.

It is surprising how few companies of reasonable size, with a number of shareholders, have a shareholders' agreement in place. Even if, as a practitioner, you are rarely asked to do a valuation, it may be rewarding nonetheless to study Chapter 13, "A Shareholders' Agreement", particularly the recommended five key provisions to be included in any agreement, and the reasons given for these. Readers may also be amused, yet informed by the practical *'Russian Roulette'* solution to a deadlocked dispute.

There is also an extensive chapter on the valuation of a professional practice (Chapter 17). This is an area that is not normally discussed in texts about valuation; indeed, there is a paucity of information or guidance on the subject. This is perhaps because professional practices have completely different structures of ownership and trading than companies. As a result, the valuation of a professional practice tends to be based on negotiations as to what is acceptable to the interested parties. *The Valuation of Businesses and Shares: A Practitioner's Perspective* provides guidelines and useful commentary in this regard.

Cases histories, not necessarily linked to the immediate text, are interspersed throughout the book. These histories are examples of circumstances commonly experienced in valuations. They illustrate that a valuation is not necessarily an end in itself; in most circumstances, the valuation is a component in a wider issue such as a dispute of some kind, the next stage being the resolution of that issue through negotiation or litigation. The valuation is the starting point of what can be the difficult resolution of the dispute in complex circumstances.

Examples of Letters of Engagement and also of Valuation Reports, vital in these days of widespread litigation, are included in the Appendices. In the experience of the author, a high percentage of negligence claims against financial advisers (accountants, investment bankers, stockbrokers, wealth managers) arise from valuation matters. A well thought-out Letter of Engagement and Valuation Report will help greatly in preventing, or at least mitigating, such claims. The essential feature here, as explained at the outset of this Foreword, is *communication with the client as to what the valuation is and as to what it is not.*

It therefore follows, of course, that no responsibility for loss occasioned to any person as a result of any material in this publication will be accepted by the author or publishers. Readers are advised to take appropriate legal, accounting and tax advice in relation to all matters discussed in this book.

Des Peelo, FCA, AITI, MCIARB

Go: An Airline Adventure, by Barbara Cassani, with Kenny Kemp (Time Warner, 2003) is a compelling book about the formation, management and sale of the low-fares subsidiary of British Airways. Go was purchased from British Airways in a venture capital-backed buyout and subsequently sold on to EasyJet. The book is recommended for anyone interested in advancing their knowledge of valuation.

Barbara Cassani's description of the advisers' approach to valuation for a possible eventual sale or flotation of Go, is revealing about the 'magic' of valuation (and disconcerting for those selling the magic, should the client get to know how simple the magic is in the circumstances).

> "Basically, for a back-of-an envelope estimate, you take profits before depreciation, financing and leasing costs and multiply it by a magic number. This estimates the value of the company before deducting your debt and the capital value of your leases. The magic number multiplier for low-cost airlines was significantly higher than for traditional carriers. The multiplier relates to how profitable the company is and whether the growth prospects look good. For airlines like British Airways it was around 7 or 8 times. For Ryanair it was over 20 times. We settled for a conservative multiplier of around 12 times – much less than EasyJet or Ryanair – and came up with a valuation of close to £1 billion in less than three years."
>
> *(Reproduced by kind permission of Barbara Cassani)*

The lesson to be taken from this is that the larger the business, the easier it is to value it. This is because the parties choose not to be involved in details, keeping it at the level of one number multiplied by another. However, the reality is much different in the great majority of valuations undertaken everyday by practitioners in the real world.

Chapter 1

The Role of the Valuer

The valuer is not an advocate on behalf of his client. Integrity, meaning objectivity, independence and impartiality, is the hallmark of the professional valuer.

The need for a valuation of a business trading as a company, or a shareholding in that company, can arise for any one of a number of reasons, including: 1–01

- A falling-out amongst shareholders
- Family succession problems
- Marital separation
- Raising venture capital
- Litigation over loss of shareholding value
- Valuations related to tax assessments
- A company buying its own shares
- Valuation prior to possible sale/purchase
- Employee shareholdings.

Types of Valuation

Broadly, there are two types of valuation, namely: 1–02

- The *'benign'* valuation, where the instructing party needs the valuation for family succession, banking purposes, an indication prior to possible sale, or similar reason.
- The *'angry'* valuation, where the instructing party is engaged in contested, often acrimonious, combat with another party.

Experienced valuers will confirm that most valuations arise in the latter, *'angry'* category. It is not always properly understood by an aggrieved party, who is instructing the valuer, that the valuation is not intended to be a measurement of his grievance. Financial advisers with limited and/or poor knowledge of valuations do not always grasp this point, producing instead a valuation to please the client.

Integrity, meaning objectivity, independence and impartiality, is the hallmark of the professional valuer. There should be no difference in the approach taken to a 'benign' or an 'angry' valuation.

1-03   At the outset, a valuer needs to be clear as to whether the valuation is to be a reasoned valuation or a non-reasoned valuation. This is sometimes referred to as a *'speaking'* or a *'non-speaking'* valuation. A non-reasoned valuation is a simple statement to the effect that in the opinion of the valuer, the value is €xxxx. Obviously, therefore, it is important that the instructing party understands that a reasoned valuation is not being provided, if such is the case.

> A UK case in 2002, *Jones v. Sherwood Computer Services Ltd*, considers the distinctions between 'speaking', and 'non-speaking' valuations, and is useful as a guide in this respect.

Experienced valuers would almost always seek not to provide a reasoned valuation. However, in many cases, the valuer will be pressured to provide a reasoned valuation, particularly where the valuation will be used in negotiations or as expert evidence in a court case. In such circumstances, it is good practice for a valuer to mark his valuation report *'Draft – without prejudice'*, or *'Draft for discussion purposes only'*, until it is clear as to the likely resolution of the matter.

1-04   In an *'angry'* valuation, there is the probability that one of the parties will not like the valuation. Hence, it seems sensible, but not always possible, for the valuer not to provide a reasoned valuation and thereby place himself in a position whereby the annoyed party nitpicks through the valuation challenging its accuracy, alleged omissions, perceived bias, and so on. It may not easily prove possible to avoid a reasoned valuation, hence the good practice suggested above at **para 1–03**.

Knowledge and Responsibility

This is not a legal or taxation textbook. Appropriate professional advice should be sought where the valuer is unsure about his instructions or matters arising from his instructions. However, the general duties and responsibilities of a valuer may be summarised as follows:

- A valuer represents himself as having the skills and knowledge which a reasonably competent member of his profession would have, as attested by other members of the profession. This would likely be interpreted in court as meaning a specialist knowledge of valuation, and not just a general knowledge of valuation common to most accountants and financial advisers.

- The valuer is not an advocate on behalf of his client.

- It is accepted that valuation is not an exact science. Two valuers may legitimately arrive at different values for the same company or shareholding. Accordingly, a valuer is not negligent simply because another valuer arrived at a different conclusion. However, a valuation, that appears to be manifestly outside an expected range of valuation may call into question the valuer's competence and the completeness and/or accuracy of the work carried out.

It is important that a valuer understands the professional responsibility involved in a valuation. All professionals owe a duty of care to their clients. It follows that they are liable for damages if negligent in carrying out their duties. In the experience of the author, a high percentage of negligence claims against financial advisers (accountants, investment bankers, stockbrokers, wealth managers) arises from valuation matters.

This liability may differ for a valuer acting as an expert as opposed to a valuer acting as an arbitrator. In general terms, a valuer acting as an expert may be sued for negligence but a valuer acting as an arbitrator may not be sued for negligence. In the latter case, the remedy for the aggrieved party is to have the arbitrator's award (i.e. the valuation) set aside if there are grounds for doing so. A valuer seeking an appointment as an arbitrator, when really acting as an expert, could be open to a subsequent legal challenge as to the validity of the appointment and/or of the award.

1–08 A Letter of Engagement with reference to the valuation, even a few paragraphs for a simple valuation, is essential to avoid misunderstandings. (Examples of Letters of Engagement are set out in **Appendix Two**.)

1–09 It is good practice to discuss beforehand the contents of the Letter of Engagement with the client. What may appear obvious or self-explanatory to a specialist valuer can be a mystery to a client with little knowledge or experience of the purpose and nature of a valuation. In some circumstances, such discussion may also help to manage the expectations of the instructing party as to the possible outcome of the valuation. This may be particularly helpful in valuation cases involving marital separation. A valuer would be wise to keep a note of any such discussions.

1–10 A valuer cannot reasonably be expected to know all aspects of a company's business. It is therefore prudent for the valuer to obtain a letter from the directors confirming that they are not aware of any foreseeable circumstances, for good or bad, that would or might have a significant effect on the future maintainable profits and/or the continuity of the company. It will not always be possible to obtain such a letter in circumstances where the directors are hostile. In these circumstances, a statement or caveat to the effect that such a confirmation was not available should be included in the valuation. (An example of a Letter of Confirmation from directors is provided in **Appendix One**.)

1–11 Often, valuations are requested as a prelude to opening negotiations as to an actual purchase/sale or a settlement between the parties. Marital separation, legal cases, and Revenue matters are obvious examples. Clients and/or their advisers may pressurise the valuer for a *'low'* or *'high'* valuation as suits their case. A valuer needs to be wary in such circumstances, particularly where valuations may be exchanged between the parties and the valuation may have to be subsequently justified in, for example, a court hearing. As explained above (see **para 1-03**) it may be advisable to mark reports as *'Draft – without prejudice'* or *'Draft for discussion purposes only'*.

Valuations are often carried out on the basis that the result will be binding on all of the parties. There are **two general exceptions** in this regard: 1-12

1. The existence of fraud or collusion would be grounds for setting aside the valuation.
2. If there is fundamental error; for example, the wrong shareholding is valued or a major matter has been misunderstood.

It is not uncommon for a party, dissatisfied with the valuation, to allege one of these exceptions in an attempt to force a different, and more favourable, valuation.

The Auditor and Valuation

The Articles of Association of many companies and many shareholders' agreements (see **Chapter 13**, A Shareholders' Agreement) state that any valuations concerning the transfer of shares in the company shall be carried out by the auditor. The premise is that the auditor has a good working knowledge of the client company and is therefore well-placed to carry out a valuation.   1-13

As mentioned earlier (**see para 1-05**), except in straightforward situations, a valuation requires specialist knowledge of valuations. An auditor therefore needs to be careful that he is not holding himself out as an expert in valuations merely because he is the auditor to the company.   1-14

It is also easy for an aggrieved outgoing shareholder, if such is the circumstance, to allege subsequent to the auditor's valuation that the auditor was biased in favour of the on-going shareholders/directors of the business.   1-15

The circumstances of the valuation can be unpleasant (such as a family row or marital separation) and the auditor will   1-16 often have personal knowledge of the parties. It is perhaps then appropriate for the auditor to diplomatically recommend that the valuation be obtained from a specialist valuer, perhaps on the premise that the auditor's independence may be challenged in court.

Circumstances of Valuation

1-17 *'Oppression of Minority'* is a phrase that regularly crops up in share valuation disputes. Section 205(1) of the Companies Act 1963 provides:

> *"Any member of a company who complains that the affairs of the company are being conducted or that the powers of the directors of the company are being exercised in a manner oppressive to him or any of the members (including himself), or in disregard of his or their interests as members, may apply to the Court for an order under this section".*

The remedies available to the court, following a successful application, include an order for the oppressor(s) to buy the petitioner(s) shares, an order the other way around, or an order for the company to be wound up.

Whether or not there is cause to support an allegation of oppression will be a matter of legal opinion. A valuer has no role in such a determination, though he may be asked to provide a valuation in the circumstances. It may be prudent for the valuer to state in his report that his valuation is not an opinion as to the validity or otherwise of the alleged oppression.

(*The Law of Private Companies* by Thomas B. Courtney (2nd Edition, Butterworths, 2002) provides a detailed review of oppression in Chapter 19, Shareholders' Remedies.)

1-18 The willingness or otherwise of the client to pay a proper fee for a valuation should not dictate the extent of the work that the valuer is willing to carry out on the valuation. (See **paras 1-08** and **1-09** and also Letters of Engagement in **Appendix Two**.)

1-19 Some business are exciting and emerging, others mundane and dull. Some businesses are new, others are mature. Each business, whilst it may have much in common with others in the same sector, has its own unique characteristics. A valuer needs to take cognisance of these factors, and should not automatically follow a formula-type valuation.

1–20 The enormous growth in available information, and ready access to it, has greatly helped valuers in their work. Statistics of all kinds, trends in industry sectors, demographics, technical data, are all now available from and at the valuer's desk.

1–21 It can be the case that a valuer is asked not to carry out a valuation of the company itself, but to apportion present and/or future value as between different shareholding interests. For example, BES investments, deferred shares, employee share schemes, etc.

1–22 Textbooks and journal articles on business and share valuations generally overlook the valuation of professional practices. Such practices are businesses, albeit not having a legal existence separate to their owners, unlike companies. The normal rules and parameters of company valuations do not apply to the valuation of professional practices. The necessity of such valuations usually arises due to retirement or to a dispute in the partnership. There are many issues, not all involving valuation, in such disputes, though a valuation may be a starting point for a resolution. (**Chapter 17** of this book is devoted entirely to the workings of professional practices and factors influencing their valuation.)

1–23 On reading the financial press or on hearing a pronouncement by the latest business guru, a valuer may sometimes feel intimidated as to his lack of knowledge about the claimed superior workings on valuation by such as investment bankers and hedge funds. It is reassuring to know that there is not always greater wisdom in the upper echelons of the financial world and that the fundamentals of valuation do not change simply because of large scale and/or complexity. (See **Salutary Tales** below.)

Salutary Tales

'Experience is the name everyone gives to their mistakes.'
Oscar Wilde

A valuation is an opinion. Hopefully, it is an informed opinion, meaning the valuation is based on known facts, careful analysis and consideration of those facts with, of course, the experience of the valuer as the final and critical factor in making the valuation.

Authoritative studies in the UK and US have repeatedly shown that a majority of acquisitions have proved disappointing and overpriced to their new owners. Obviously, the price paid was based on somebody, somewhere, making a valuation and then persuading others of its validity. This phenomenon of disappointment and overpricing appears to be more prevalent in large companies, which, paradoxically, would appear to have the best of advice and experience available to them.

- An international survey carried out in 2006 on behalf of KPMG concluded that more than two thirds of company takeovers failed to add value for the company making the acquisition.

- In February 2005, *Time* magazine reported that in seven of the nine mergers valued at more than US$50 billion the acquirer's share price was subsequently down on average by 46% from pre-merger levels.

- Two great pillars of the UK industrial establishment, Marconi (formerly GEC) and Imperial Chemical Industries (ICI), reduced themselves to minor shadows of their former selves with poorly researched takeovers.

- Vodafone had a write-down of US$48 billion relating to its takeover of Mannesmann in 2000.

- The largest merger ever in US history, Time Warner and AOL, ended with the write-off of AOL in its entirety.

History repeats itself in that the principal concerns in making acquisitions appear to have been a concentration on the size of the acquisition (as large as possible), and the sophistication of the financial arrangements (which the directors did not understand), and that the actual transaction is driven by investment bankers, the most basic fundamentals of valuation being obviously unknown to the bankers or management.

Time and again, it has been demonstrated subsequent to the acquisition that nobody could properly explain how they valued the acquisition in the first place.

Chapter 2

The Fundamentals of Valuation

It is fundamental that what is being valued is the right to receive future income, that future income being profits and/or capital appreciation, and the valuation being what a purchaser would likely pay to receive that income. Valuation is always future-oriented.

2-01   A valuation is a best estimate of the price a purchaser would pay for a company or a shareholding in the company, at a particular time. As explained at different points in this book, the definition of the purchaser, and the circumstances of the valuation, will be significant influences on the price. It is not true to say that one valuation fits all circumstances.

It is also important to understand that the principles of valuation are the same for small and large companies. The principles apply equally to the valuation of a modest business or to Global Enterprises Plc, no matter what complex 'financial engineering' may be involved.

2-02   Most valuations are carried out on the basis of a hypothetical sale. In effect, the valuation posits a figure that would apply in the event that the particular business or shareholding was sold. It is a common fallacy that a valuation is an arithmetical process in that a business can be adequately and reasonably valued by simply multiplying the latest after-tax profits by a profit multiple (P/E) obtained from general comparative data, as if such a multiple covers all the realities of the particular business.

2-03   The reason itself for the valuation may have an influence. That is why a number of the chapters in this book are devoted to some specific circumstances of valuation, such as a falling-out amongst shareholders or claims that a quasi-partnership exists. Other chapters cover specific aspects of valuation, such as a minority shareholding or particular methods of valuation.

No matter what spin, jargon or suggestion of mysterious expertise in valuation is put forward, it is fundamental that what is being valued is the **right to receive future income,** that future income being profits and/or capital appreciation. The valuation is what a purchaser would likely pay to receive that income. **Valuation is always future-oriented.**

2-04

Common Errors

Sometimes, on reading press reports or hearing commentaries on radio, television, at seminars, and so on, it seems that picking a *'multiple'* is the only key element to valuation. A multiple means that the valuation is calculated on a number of times the annual profits. This can be true, but in most cases it is not the complete picture. It is advisable also, to recognise that the size of a business also greatly influences the multiple. In general, smaller businesses have smaller multiples in valuation than larger businesses, the reasons for which are explained later in this book. (See **Chapter 9**, Valuing a Small Business.)

2-05

The most common error in private company valuations is to regard press reports on sales of large companies, or stock market multiple comparisons, as being universally applicable to the valuation of small and medium-sized companies.

Financial advisers (accountants, investment bankers, stockbrokers, wealth managers) are frequently asked informally about the valuation of a particular business in the mistaken belief by the questioner that there is some simple answer such as *'well, businesses like yours are selling for x time profits'*. Sometimes too, the questioner has picked up some *'rule of thumb'* regarding his particular business sector, e.g. *'the value is twice turnover, isn't it?'* This sort of question can be difficult to handle for the adviser as the expected answer seems straightforward to the questioner. As explained later in this book, *'rules of thumb'* are unwise as an absolute method of valuation. (See **Chapter 7**, Rules of Thumb.)

2-06

Judgement

2-07 If an investor wishes to buy shares in a quoted company (a public company quoted on the stock market) the position is relatively clear, insofar as the shares may be readily purchased at the stockmarket price of the day. Buying a large shareholding in a quoted company, or to taking over the entire company, would require a different and higher price. While there is no advance certainty as to what such a price might be, there are usually stock market precedents and comparisons available to assist such a determination.

Studies in the UK have indicated that a premium of between 30% and 50%, over the pre-bid stockmarket price, is necessary to acquire an entire company.

2-08 The position in a private company (sometimes referred to as an 'unquoted company') is entirely different to a quoted company. There is no market price available as a guide. The law and practice relating to the valuation of a private company, or a shareholding in it, is quite different from that for a quoted company. Frequently, a valuation has to be made in a vacuum as there will probably be no comparable precedent or recent transaction in the shares of the private company. In any event, the circumstances of the valuation, and of the company itself, are usually sufficiently unique in themselves to make it unlikely that a reasonably comparable precedent can be found.

2-09 The ownership of a private company, whether the whole company or a shareholding, will almost inevitably change hands over a period of time (except for subsidiaries of larger companies) whether through outright sale, death of a shareholder, family succession, a shareholders' dispute, a change in circumstances, and so on.

2-10 It is often said, and with some validity, that ultimately a share valuation is a question of negotiation between the interested parties. It can be true as well to say that a particular company or shareholding may have different values to different people at different times. It is also true that two financial advisers may legitimately arrive at different values for the same company or shareholding, which suggests that such valuations are simply a matter of judgement and/or negotiation within wide parameters and which pay little regard to any techniques of measurement or appraisal.

The reality is different as, while there is no doubt that valuations are dependent on judgement, the parameters of valuation are narrower than might be immediately apparent, having been determined by case law and Revenue practice over the years, as well as by a general convergence of opinion by experienced valuation practitioners. **2–11**

It is important to recognise that the law regarding valuation tends to focus on what a purchaser is willing to pay rather than what a seller is willing to accept.

Company Law

It is necessary, in making a valuation, to have a good understanding of company law relating to private companies. The level of voting shareholding is a critical factor, as company law provides different rights for different percentages of shareholding. (The valuation of non-voting shares is referred to in **para 2–49**.) **2–12**

A voting shareholding (or combined shareholdings) of 50% plus one share appoints the directors and decides whether or not to pay a dividend. A shareholding of less than 50% does not in itself, no matter the size, entitle the shareholder to be a director or to be consulted by the directors.

A voting shareholding (or combined shareholdings) of 75% or more is required to pass what is known in company law as a *'Special Resolution'*. In reality, the power of such a shareholding refers to the ability to alter the Articles of Association or to wind up the company. It follows that a voting shareholding (or combined shareholdings) of more than 25% has the power to block a Special Resolution. **2–13**

All companies are required by law to have a Memorandum of Association and Articles of Association. The former refers to the purpose or objects of the company. In practice, these definitions are usually so widely drawn that the company can engage in **2–14** almost any business or activity. The Articles of Association, normally referred to simply as 'the Articles', cover the legal structure of the company as to the rights and entitlements of different classes of shares, the powers of directors, ability to borrow, and so on.

(Two noteworthy textbooks on Irish Company Law are: Ronan Keane, *Company Law* (4th Edition, Tottel, 2007), and Thomas B. Courtney, *The Law of Private Companies* (2nd Edition, Butterworths, 2002).)

2–15 Most private companies adopt standard Articles as set down in the Companies Acts, and which may be amended to suit specific circumstances. Some Articles are extremely complicated. Standard Articles do not set out a basis for valuing shareholdings in the company as this would not normally be included in the Articles. In a small number of older companies, the Articles specify a basis of valuation to be followed for the transfer of shareholdings. Such provisions usually say that the auditor must carry out the valuation regarding any transfers, occasionally including complex formulae to do so, but commonly referring to the valuation basis being, e.g. *'fair value'* or *'market value'*. Today, the practice is to include the basis of valuation, if required, in a separate shareholders' agreement rather than in the Articles. (See **Chapter 14**, Fair Value, Market Value and Willing Buyer/Willing Seller.)

2–16 It should be understood, that a *'true'* valuation may be quite different than a valuation computed by following a definition set out in the Articles or in a shareholders' agreement. A *'true'* valuation should be a best estimate of what a prospective purchaser would be likely to pay for the shareholding. If the instructions to the valuer are to follow a particular definition or valuation basis, this must be followed. The valuer should make it clear in his valuation report that such is the case.

2–17 A shareholders' agreement (a legally binding written agreement to ensure equality, or agreed arrangements, between shareholders) may exist and where it does exist it will likely include a basis of valuation for the transfer or sale of shareholdings in the company. (See **Chapter 13**, A Shareholders' Agreement.)

It follows that the first step in completing a valuation of a shareholding (as opposed to valuing the entire business, in which case the Articles and/or a shareholders' agreement will almost certainly be irrelevant) is to read the Articles and shareholders' agreement, if any, to ascertain what rights and entitlements attach to the shareholding, as these can influence the valuation. There may be different classes of shares, different entitlements to dividends, entitlements to assets on a winding-up, and similar provisions.

2–18

A Minority Shareholding

The most vexed question in valuations is the position of a minority shareholder. This is the cause of most problems and disputes amongst shareholders and is frequently the reason for the valuation in the first place.

2–19

In the absence of any clear instructions or agreement to the contrary, the shareholding should be valued for what it is, a minority shareholding with all the restrictions that go with that status. It is not for the valuer to decide otherwise.

It can be disconcerting to those not versed in company law to discover that few rights and entitlements, in terms of participation in the decisions affecting the company, attach to a minority shareholding. A minority shareholding is not completely without such rights, but those rights are quite restricted. It can also be a surprise to discover that these restrictions in themselves are not a cause for an oppression action by the minority against the majority, unless the restrictions are used in blatant disregard of the interests of the minority. It is not the role of the valuer to decide what is, or is not, oppression; that decision is for legal advice and for the courts. (See **para 1–17** regarding 'oppression of minority'.)

2–20

As explained above (see **para 2–12**), the majority shareholders have unrestricted rights as to the appointment of all directors, and on whether or not to pay a dividend, and they may run the company without reference to the minority shareholders,

2–21

except for the requirements of the Companies Acts regarding the provision of audited accounts and the holding of general meetings.

2-22 A minority shareholder, subject to legal advice in particular circumstances, is in effect *'locked-in'* unless and until the directors approve (in terms of the registration of a new shareholder) the sale of his shareholding to other shareholders or to an approved outsider, or the entire company is sold. It is also the case (unless the Articles or shareholders' agreement say otherwise) that the majority shareholding may be sold to a third party without reference to the minority shareholder, and that the former is under no legal obligation to obtain a similar offer for the minority shareholders. It might be noted, however, that under company law, an outside party acquiring 80% or more of the shareholding in a company can compulsorily acquire (if the outside party wishes – there is no obligation) the minority shareholders at the same pro-rata price as paid to the 80% or more shareholder(s).

2-23 It follows, because of these restrictions, that a minority shareholding has a different, and lower, proportionate valuation than a majority shareholding. For example, a 20% shareholding would not necessarily have a valuation equal to one-third of the valuation for a 60% shareholding in the same company. The total valuations of the individual shareholdings in a company (valued in isolation of each other, depending on the spread of shareholdings) will probably not add up to the value of the company as an entire entity.

The spread of shareholdings may mean that a minority shareholding may be part of a possible combined majority shareholding. For example, shareholdings such as 40:40:20%, or 45:45:10% or even 49:49:2%. (See **paras 2-34** and **2-35**.)

Shareholdings and Voting Influence in a Company

% SHAREHOLDING	VOTING INFLUENCE
0–10%	Little, if any, unless it holds the balance of power
10–25%	Little, but depends on spread/percentage of other shareholdings
25% + one share or more	Can prevent winding-up or an amendment to the Articles
50%	Deadlock, but depends on attitude of other shareholder(s)
50% + one share or more	Appoints directors and decides their remuneration. Decides dividends
75%	Absolute control. Can wind-up company or amend the Articles
80%	Can compulsorily purchase remaining shareholdings

Note: shareholders may combine their shareholdings to achieve the above percentages.

2-24 A minority shareholding is normally valued at a discount to its percentage proportion of the valuation of the company as an entire entity. This is commonly referred to as *'minority discount'*, and is explained later in this book (see **Chapter 5**, The Minority Position.)

Income and Valuation

2-25 Other than a transaction of a short-term or speculative nature, an investment is made in the expectation of generating an income over a period in the future, the price paid for the investment being the capitalised value of that expected future income. **Valuation is about estimating that price.**

2-26 This concept, or underlying theory of investment, does not ignore the possibility of capital appreciation insofar as the price paid for the investment should reflect this possibility.

> **EXAMPLE**
>
> To receive a gross income (i.e. interest) of €100 from government bonds (known as *'gilts'*) would require an investment of €2,500 (assuming that interest rates are 4%), whereas to receive a gross income (i.e. dividends) of €100 from a leading quoted company would likely require an investment (known as investment in *'equities'*) in the region of €5,000 (assuming general dividend yields are around 2%).

2-27 The difference between the foregoing investments of €2,500 and €5,000 is that unlike, the investment in gilts, the investment in equities reflects the possibility of a growing income and hence capital appreciation. **The marketplace will always pay a higher price for the possibility of growth in the capital value of the investment.**

2-28 This confirms the earlier assertion (see **para 2-04**) that a fundamental feature of valuation is that the **right to receive future income** is what is being valued. Future income in this context includes profits/dividends and capital appreciation.

2-29 **The valuation of a shareholding in a private company, whether majority or minority, is primarily dependent upon the income which the shareholding can be reasonably expected to provide so far as can be reasonably foreseen at the date of valuation.**

2-30 Ascertaining just what the income for that shareholding may be and then placing a capitalised value (i.e. multiple) on that income, are the two most fundamental steps in making a valuation. The capitalised value is known as an *'earnings valuation'*.

There will be circumstances where the valuation is not straightforward. For example, a loss-making company, a company where there are strong assets but poor profitability, a complex share structure, and so on. There are various case histories in this book dealing with these circumstances.

Income for a majority shareholding is usually taken as the company's profits (on the premise that the majority shareholder has control over the use of those profits) compared with a minority shareholding which, in theory, should be valued on the basis of the dividend (the only income available to such a shareholder if dividends are being paid). Dividends are dependent upon profits, so the second stage of a valuation is, in any event, to look to the profits position. The first stage is a review of the rights and entitlements attaching to the shareholding. These will be set out in the Articles, as amended by any shareholders' agreement.

There is often confusion in the terms used for 'profits' in valuations. *'Future maintainable profits'* is now generally taken as net-of-tax profits. References to *'earnings'*, as usually referring to quoted companies, also means (historical) net-of-tax profits. In private company valuations, *'future maintainable profits'* is generally the term used. (In this book, references to profits, unless stated otherwise, are to net-of-tax profits.)

The dividend method of valuing minority shareholdings, while still valid, is now largely replaced by a method using discounted total company valuations. This reflects the reality that dividends are now rarely paid in small to medium-sized companies. Large private companies sometimes pay regular dividends but usually at levels lower than justified by profits.

Case History: A Minority Valuation

A subsidiary of a major food processing and distribution group was 80% owned by the parent and 20% by the managing director. The managing director had sold the 80% some seven years previously. Relations between the parties had deteriorated with the parent alleging poor management and a counter allegation that the parent had restricted the development of the subsidiary to its own advantage elsewhere in the group. A section 205 Companies Act 1963 legal action regarding alleged oppression of minority ensued.

A valuer (on behalf of the 20% shareholder) used future maintainable net-of-tax profits some 40% higher than the actual net-of-tax profits on the basis that such represented the estimated *'true'* profits, had the development of the company not been restricted and that group management charges to the subsidiary were excessive. The parent company responded that the actual net-of-tax profits were overstated as the subsidiary had benefited from a substantial interest-free loan that had grown over the years, and received the benefit of group services at less than *'true'* cost.

It transpired that the parent company had made two acquisitions and a disposal of a business during the previous 18 months, at multiples of net-of-tax profits in the range of 8–10 times. These were significantly larger businesses than the particular subsidiary.

The compromise settlement, made immediately prior to the hearing of the case, was a valuation of seven times actual net-of-tax profits, without any of the claimed adjustments, and no discount for minority. (**Note:** in court-related settlements, there is usually a distortion in the valuation due to the buying-off, for greater or lesser value, of the risk and costs involved in a full court hearing.)

It is difficult to avoid subjective judgement in estimating future maintainable profits, but in doing so the valuer must recall that the purpose is to quantify the likely future maintainable profits, not to judge the risk of the investment. The capitalised value, or to put it differently, the multiple of profits, should reflect the risk attaching to the investment.

2–32

In broad terms, the higher the risk, the lower the multiple. Risk in this context means the chance of losing some or all of the investment, whether through lower future profitability or the business failing altogether. All businesses are risky but some are riskier than others.

Reference was made earlier (see **para 2–06**) to *'rules of thumb'*. Common examples of these are pubs being valued on a multiple of turnover, hotels on a per room basis, insurance brokers on a multiple of annual commissions, convenience stores at number of weeks' turnover, etc.

2–33

Experience suggests that 'rules of thumb' tend to result in the over-valuation of businesses, as the highest 'rule of thumb' is usually quoted. For example, the sale of a five-star 'trophy' hotel is used as a basis of valuation or measurement for other hotels, or an unusually high sales price for a company is held out as a new 'norm' for valuations in that particular business sector. (See **Chapter 7**, Rules of Thumb.)

Spread of Shareholdings

The spread of shareholdings may have an impact on a valuation. It is not unusual in a private company to have a number of shareholdings, none of which is a majority. In such cases, there may be what is known as an *'influential minority'*, such as a shareholding of 40% where there are three other shareholdings of 20% each.

2–34

There may also be what is known as a *'ransom'* shareholding. A 2% shareholder where there are two 49% shareholdings is an extreme example. There is also an element of *'ransom'* in shareholdings of 20:40:40%, 10:45:45%, and so on. The smallest shareholding therein may have a valuation well in excess of its otherwise discounted minority valuation.

2–35

2-36 In many small and medium-sized companies the shareholders and management are one and the same. Such businesses are often critically dependent on the continuity of a key individual or individuals. This factor may have an influence on the valuation, particularly in circumstances of a valuation arising from sudden change, such as the death or resignation of a key individual.

Net Assets and Valuation

2-37 A valuation arrived at on the basis of expected future income capitalised at the appropriate multiple may have little relationship to the value of the underlying net assets. Net assets are defined as the gross assets (using updated values for property) less the gross liabilities. Net assets are described as *'Shareholders' Funds'* on the balance sheet, using updated asset values where appropriate. Where this net asset value is materially different from the capitalised value, this raises the issue of whether or not this factor should be taken into account in the valuation. (See **Chapter 6**, The Role of Assets.)

2-38 It may be that there are surplus assets in the company and the valuer needs to be careful to identify any such assets. A common example is a company with significant cash balances/investments (and nil or small borrowings) on its balance sheet. A valuer should establish if such cash/investments, or at least a proportion of them, are surplus to the requirements of the business (there may be seasonal swings in cash balances). The income from these assets (such as interest, rent and dividends) is excluded from future maintainable pre-tax profits, and the value of these assets is then added to the separate valuation of the underlying business.

General Indication of Value

2-39 There is a growing tendency, particularly where a dispute or litigation is involved, for specialist valuers to express valuations in less precise terms such as:

> *'in the region of €xxxxxx'*
> *'in excess of €xxxxxx'*
> *'in the range of €x to €xxxxxx'*

This trend perhaps reflects the wariness of the valuer to being queried or cross-examined in court should he provide a more precise valuation.

2-40 It is often the case that the necessity of a valuation can arise quickly and is expected to be completed with little information provided beyond the Articles and the latest audited accounts. In such circumstances, the valuer can only scan the accounts and adjust for any obvious anomaly or unusual aspect. He must also expect that his own general knowledge of the business sector is sufficient to have a reasonable understanding of the likely continuity of profits. Such a valuation is sometimes referred to as a *'desk valuation'*, or *'indicative valuation'* being akin to what are referred to as *'drive-by valuations'* by property valuers.

The valuer should make clear in his report the limited nature of his valuation and the basis on which it is prepared. It is good practice to describe the valuation as *'a general indication of value'*.

2-41 No amount of explanation and detailed examples could exhaustively cover the topic of business and share valuations. It is only in the most complex situations that there is likely to be disagreement amongst experienced practitioners as to the **approach** to valuation. There may be disagreement on future maintainable profits, the appropriate multiple, the discount factor, etc., but rarely is there disagreement as to the principles of valuation involved.

2-42 There are many different judgements involved in making a valuation and there is, therefore, scope for differences of opinion. These differences become more focused, and much less contested, where there is the prospect of an actual sale or purchase. The contemplation or prospect of money brings reality to valuation.

Alternative Valuations

2-43 This book does not purport to cover circumstances of share complexity, theorems of markets, mathematical analyses, fine legal issues, and the valuation of *'financial engineering'* type shareholdings (such as warrants, complex options, deferred shares, etc.).

These issues only occasionally arise in Irish circumstances. For guidance, should such an issue arise, there are two noteworthy

UK text books that cover these topics, namely: *Tolley's Practical Share and Business Valuation* by David Bowes (LexisNexis, 2008) and Christopher Glover, *The Valuation of Unquoted Companies* (5th Edition, CCH, 2009).

2-44 The recurring theme in this book is that a valuation is a best estimate of the price a purchaser would pay for a company or a shareholding in the company at a particular date. The assumption that a purchaser is available, even when the valuation is made on a willing buyer/willing seller basis, has to be tempered by the reality that any purchaser always has the choice of spending his money on a different investment. Hence, a valuation is always a competitive process in terms of comparisons with the alternative use of monies.

2-45 The alternative use of monies includes the fact, often overlooked in valuations, that a potential purchaser (particularly a purchaser with knowledge of the business sector involved) could always choose instead to set up in competition. A potential purchaser, properly advised, will usually have privately completed some evaluation in this regard.

It would not normally be the role of the valuer to carry out such an evaluation as part of a *'due diligence'* or a review of information process. However, common sense and the experience of the valuer will dictate the extent to which a business sector is *'easy entry'*, and accordingly make an allowance for this factor in the valuation. (See **para 3-16** on *'pricing power'*.)

2-46 The paramount method of business and share valuation is the earnings valuation (see **para 2-30**). Net assets may have an influence on a valuation but is rarely a method of valuation in itself, except for passive property and/or investment-owning companies (**para 6-11**). (See **Chapter 6**, The Role of Assets.)

From time to time, there are attempts in some way or other to take away or diminish the judgement aspect of valuation and instead introduce some mathematical process (such as Discounted Cash Flows or 'DCF') or an apparently sophisticated method (e.g. EBITDA) into valuations. Neither of these methods has impacted on valuation practice in any meaningful way.

(These processes are further explained in **Chapter 10**, regarding Discounted Cash Flows, and on page 53 regarding EBITDA.)

Companies with positive cash flows are more attractive, and generally more highly valued, than companies with committed cash flows. For example, a supermarket chain making €10 million in annual net-of-tax profits will likely have that money in the bank at financial year-end; a widget manufacturer making the same profits will likely have a significant amount of these profits tied-up in increased net working capital, meeting the need for new/replacement of plant and machinery, etc. 2–47

Complexity

As illustrated by the case histories throughout this book, some valuations can be quite complex. On occasion, the valuation can be no more than an indication of value (probably setting out a range of possible values) to allow and/or to progress negotiations towards providing solutions for the complex issues involved. 2–48

A valuation may involve voting and non-voting ordinary shares. Where this happens (often in family-owned businesses) and the shares are otherwise *'pari passu'*, it is accepted practice to allocate a premium of 15% to the value of the voting shares. The Revenue Commissioners adopt this approach in such circumstances (see **Appendix Four**). More complex circumstances involving non-voting shares would have to be assessed on their merits. 2–49

Working Papers

A valuation is not the outcome of an investigation, nor is it an audit. A valuer, in his Letter of Engagement (see **Appendix Two**), will have stated the extent of his reliance on provided information (such as the audited accounts). As explained at **paras 1–05** and **1–06**, the valuer carries professional responsibilities that may not always be limited by what is stated in a Letter of Engagement. It is essential for a valuer to have working papers to demonstrate that he has followed good practice in making his valuation. 2–50

A basic checklist/review that a valuer should be able to demonstrate in his working papers is set out below. (See 'An Outline Due Diligence Review' on page 34.)

Basic Checklist / Review for Valuation Working Papers

- Review the Articles of Association regarding:
  (a) any basis of valuation set out therein
  (b) rights and entitlements attaching to different (if any) classes of shareholdings
  (c) unusual clauses that may affect valuations.

- Review shareholders' agreements, if any, regarding:
  (a) any basis of valuation set out therein
  (b) rights and entitlements attaching to different (if any) classes of shareholdings
  (c) unusual clauses that may affect valuations.

- Obtain written confirmation from the directors setting out:
  (a) details of any transactions in the shares of the company within the previous five years
  (b) the existence and details of any share options
  (c) details of any shares held in trust by any of the shareholders.

- Obtain copies of the complete audited accounts for the latest three financial years, including audited accounts for each subsidiary and associated company.

- Obtain copies of up-to-date management accounts (these may not always be available).

- Check the audited and management accounts for unusual or non-recurring items of expense or income included in the accounts.

- Review the accounting policies and notes to the accounts. A review can, on occasion, show up, e.g. inadequate depreciation policies, inconsistent research and development policies, overstated directors' valuations of assets, loans or investments that are not recoverable, and so on.

- Review the balance sheet for surplus assets. This should include under-utilised assets, such as a valuable property that could be replaced by a lesser property.
- Review key personnel in terms of their importance to the continuity of the business and general well-being of the company.
- Obtain written confirmation from the directors that, save as disclosed, there are no known or foreseeable major factors that will influence the continuity and/or profitability of the business for good or bad.

Case History: The Withdrawal of an Agency

A distribution company held the agency in Ireland for a leading range of branded consumer products. The agency, held for 15 years, comprised 70% of the business, with much of the remaining 30% being other products that 'piggy-backed' on the branded products into supermarkets and other retail outlets. An international merger between two very large companies, including the branded products' owner, resulted in the company losing the agency as the distribution was switched and amalgamated with the existing distributor in Ireland for the other parent company.

The company sued for loss on the basis that the result was the loss of the entire company and accordingly this could be measured by a valuation of the business (meaning a loss to the shareholders). There were legal difficulties in this approach (even assuming liability was established) including the conflict that: on one hand the company itself, and not the (once-removed) shareholders had suffered loss; and, on the other hand, where the loss was virtually total (as claimed) there was no difference between the interests of the shareholders and the company itself.

It was also argued that the present-day value of the expected future profits stream would largely equate to a valuation based on a multiple of these profits (which, in strict theory, was correct). The company claimed it could not reasonably have mitigated its loss having regard to its near total dependence on the one brand of products.

The valuation approach to loss was not accepted by the court. Instead, two years' loss of pre-tax profits was awarded on the grounds that, in any event, the vagaries of business could have resulted in the loss of the agency for any number of reasons, but reasonable notice thereof was required in the particular circumstances.

Chapter 3

Future Maintainable Profits

There is no certainty in business forecasts.

3–01 The right to receive future income is what is being valued, valuation being future-oriented. The assessment of income for the purpose of valuation starts with future maintainable profits. In a private company valuation, this means net-of-tax profits. (see **para 2–31**.)

3–02 Inevitably, it is quite impossible to estimate, except in the most stable of situations, the expected profits position beyond two or three years hence. Forecasts beyond that often lack credibility. In practice, for the purpose of valuation, the profits for the current financial year are usually calculated together with more outline estimates of the position for one or two years ahead. (This lack of credibility is a major drawback to valuations based on Discount Cash Flows (DCF). See **Chapter 10**.)

3–03 It is necessary to check carefully for unusual or non-recurring items of expense or income included in the audited accounts (and in management accounts, where applicable), and to make adjustments accordingly. These are usually obvious on year-to-year comparisons of the profit and loss accounts. Nevertheless, due enquiry should be made as to the possible existence of any such items, which may not be obvious. For example, a major customer may have been gained or lost, or a product line introduced or discontinued. (See **para 1–10** regarding Letter of Confirmation from the directors. See also **para 3–15** on '*due diligence*'.)

3–04 Few companies have orderly or progressive trends in profitability. Many businesses have one exceptionally good year or bad year in every period of four or five years. Why this happens is not always apparent but it is surprisingly common. Some sectors are cyclical, such as construction, suppliers of capital goods (plant and machinery, heavy vehicles), packaging etc. Other sectors, such as tourism and agriculture, have erratic records.

Average of Profits

3-05 The application of a weighted average to historical profits in order to estimate future maintainable profits is common valuation practice for companies with erratic profit histories. Here is a simplified example:

EXAMPLE

Amounts in Euro

Net-of-tax Profits

Year 1	212,419	x	1	=	212,419
Year 2	174,838	x	2	=	349,676
Year 3	247,988	x	3	=	743,964
(latest year)					
	Totals		6		1,306,059

1,306,059 / 6 = 217,676 = **weighted average annual net-of-tax profits**

The use of a weighted average is not a perfect system for estimating future profits, but often it is the best available method in the circumstances. Note that the heaviest weighting is given to the latest year. Occasionally, in a relatively stable business, though with cyclical aspects, a longer period of five years might be used.

3-06 A simple average of profits over the latest three financial years, or possibly over five on rare occasions, might be more appropriate than a weighed average in circumstances where the fluctuations year-on-year are relatively minor and there is little growth. There is no 'norm' as to which method (weighted or simple average) is best for particular circumstances. This is a matter for judgement by the valuer.

There is no Certainty in Business Forecasts

"It is economic forecasting that makes astrology respectable."
John Kenneth Galbraith

Estimating likely future profits is fraught with difficulties. Many companies have erratic profit records or the prospects may be significantly better or worse than the historical performance suggests. The future risk to profits has to be assessed on three levels, namely:

- The macro outlook, meaning the foreseeable national outlook, including overseas markets where relevant. This may include assessment of currency risk.

- Sectoral risk, meaning companies dependent on trends in particular sectors, such as construction, agriculture or tourism.

- The general risk of the business itself. For example, product obsolescence or dependence on key customers and/or suppliers.

A common error or fallacy in estimating future profits is to thoughtlessly extrapolate a historical profits progression into an assessment of future profits. This is no more than meaningless *'number crunching'*. The mathematics of previous profit progressions (meaning the annual percentage growth measured over previous years) is an historical outcome and not a perceived certainty, or a reasonable assumption, as to future performance.

It is also the case that, in such circumstances, the percentage growth is being applied to a higher and higher base figure.

The Purchaser and Synergy

3-07 A potential purchaser of a business may adopt a different approach to ascertaining future profits, by instead estimating the future profits under the new ownership. Such a purchaser may feel able to pay a higher than normal price for a business on the grounds that the purchaser can bring added profits to the acquired business by eliminating duplicated costs, applying economies of scale, cross-selling to the newly acquired customers, and so on. This approach to valuation (if carried through in an increased purchase price) is erroneous, as the purchaser is then in effect paying the vendor an enhanced price for the addition of the purchaser's own opportunity and expertise.

3-08 Conversely, the purchaser of a business must be careful that it is not in fact bringing increased costs, and hence reduced future profits, to the newly acquired business. Experience has shown that this can occur particularly when a large well-known company acquires a smaller company in the same business. Subsequent demands for pay and benefit parity with employees in the large company, the cost of upgrading processes, systems, etc. or even adapting the 'culture' of the smaller company to the higher standard of the acquiring company, can erode the expected future profits.

Stability and Volatility

3-09 In estimating future profits, it is instructive to note that some sectors/companies are stable and grow by accretion due to steady repeat business. A supermarket is an obvious example, where the same customers provide the same business every week. A branded consumer product can generate customer loyalty, as can location (such as being the only warehouse provider near to a particular port or an airport). There is not the constant need to find new replacement customers in such businesses. Short-term gains or losses of customers, barring catastrophe, tend to be marginal in number.

3-10 In contrast, other sectors, such as construction and engineering contractors, machinery manufacturers, textiles sub-contractors, and so on, are less certain repeat business, in many cases being subject to sectoral volatility and/or of competitive tendering processes. There may also only be a small number of customers available in the particular sector or market.

The Use of Profits

The estimated future profits normally provide the basis for valuing a majority shareholding, on the basis that the owner of such a shareholding can dictate the use of those profits to his own advantage.   3–11

A minority shareholder, in contrast, is not in that position and, in the absence of special circumstances (such as a shareholders' agreement), has no influence over the amount of profits that may be distributed as dividends. On this premise (See **para 2–31**), the valuation attributable to a minority shareholding is the probable future dividend capitalised (multiplied) at the appropriate rate. The trend is, however, to value a minority shareholding on the same basis as a majority shareholding, but at varying levels of discount.   3–12

(See **paras 5–03** to **5–12** regarding dividend valuations.)

Reliance on Accounts

In assessing future maintainable profits, the valuer will primarily rely on audited accounts. The valuer would be unwise to rely on audited accounts more than nine months out-of-date as representing up-to-date complete financial information. The trading and financial circumstances of a business can change quickly through, for example, the gain or loss of a major customer, currency movements, and so on.   3–13

(A simple analysis of the latest balance sheet can also reveal much about the foreseeable financial risk to the continuity of the business. See page 37 for an example of such an analysis.)

A question arises as to reliance by a valuer on management accounts. The following observations can be made in this regard: 3–14

- The management accounts (for whatever number of months) may reflect a seasonal business, meaning that the period involved may reflect the best or worst months of the financial year.

- Management accounts produced on an irregular or unstructured basis must be treated with extreme caution, particularly if produced in the context of assisting a share valuation.

- Regular management accounts carried through to full balance sheets are a good indication of reliability.
- The acid test on reliability is a comparison of past management accounts with the audited accounts for the same financial year.

Due Diligence

3–15 Most valuations are straightforward where the available financial information is reasonably reliable. In more complex situations, the valuer has to make a judgement as to the amount of confirmatory or *'due diligence'* work that should be undertaken prior to valuation. There are two types of due diligence, namely commercial due diligence (meaning a review of the products, the continuity/dependence on particular customers, the dependence on currency exchange rates, etc.) and financial due diligence (meaning the ability of the business to finance itself, gross profit margins, likely changes in expenses, etc.). An outline due diligence review, useful as a general checklist, is given below.

(Two useful UK textbooks in this regard are: Vanessa Williams, *Due Diligence: A Practical Guide* (Jordans, 2008) and Peter Howson, *Commercial Due Diligence: The Key to Understanding Value in an Acquisition* (Gower, 2006).) The Irish Taxation Institute publishes *Buying and Selling a Business: Tax and Legal Issues*. This book includes the Dublin Solicitors' Bar Association (DSBA) Specimen Share Purchase Agreement. Note that this Agreement was recently updated (2009) by the DSBA.)

AN OUTLINE DUE DILIGENCE REVIEW

The products/services of the business, the very bedrock of the enterprise, should be reviewed very carefully. Is a need developing for a new or an updated product? Most products/services are at least partly outdated, if not redundant, within five years. Heavy development or re-development costs may have to be faced before long.

- A close look at the nature and age of the fixed assets (plant, machinery, equipment) may show a near requirement for replacement, with consequent higher depreciation and finance charges.

Significant agreements may be due to run out and/or be subject to renewal, with possible impacts on profits. Examples include: rent reviews, sales or agency agreements, intellectual property protections, licensing arrangements, and so on.

- The impact of currency movements, whether in dealings with suppliers or customers, may have distorted (for good or bad) past and/or current profits. A surprising number of companies in apparently passive trades are vulnerable to significant currency movements, often indirectly through currency pressures on their suppliers and/or customers.

- Directors' remuneration may be excessive in the circumstances. Besides being a subjective judgement, an adjustment for any such excess in making a minority valuation can be awkward, as it may be interpreted as confirmation of oppression by the majority in taking undue reward at the expense of the minority.

- Directors' remuneration may be understated. For example, remuneration is instead taken by repayment of an outstanding loan by the director(s) to the company, or the directors obtain their income elsewhere.

- Adjustment for any benefit arising from a third-party relationship, such as favourable trading terms from an associated company, transfer pricing with an associated company, or an interest-free loan from a parent or associated company. Sometimes such a relationship can be unfavourable, if it involves, for example, excessive management charges, or adverse trading structures for tax reasons.

Pricing Power

What is known as *'pricing power'* is increasingly recognised as an important component of business success, that is, the ability or otherwise to dictate the product or service price to the marketplace. Obviously, this 'power' can greatly influence profitability. Its relevance to valuation is that a valuer should consider 'pricing power' in the context of assessing both future maintainable profits and the applicable multiple in valuation.

3-17 What 'pricing power' really means is the ability to exclude, or at least restrict, competition for a product or service for which there is a demand in the marketplace. The strategic advantage involved, meaning the ability to dictate price to advantage, may be one or more of the following:

- Ownership of intellectual property such as a patent or copyright
- Advanced integrated technology not easily replicated
- Heavy and/or prolonged entry costs for a competitor
- Monopoly or quasi-monopoly through exclusive licence, regulation or similar
- Strong skills in product innovation and/or substantial investment in product marketing support
- Strong management record on quality of service.

3-18 **The important aspect of 'pricing power' in valuation is the assessment as to whether or not it can be sustained into the foreseeable future.**

FUTURE MAINTAINABLE PROFITS 3-18

A Simple Analysis of a Balance Sheet

(This balance sheet, in Euro thousands, is for a widget manufacturing business selling its output on credit. The analysis is on the next page.)

ASSETS OF THE BUSINESS

Fixed assets:	Premises	860	This is what the company paid for the premises five years ago
Fixed assets:	Plant and machinery	790	This is the cost of the P&M, less 10% pa for depreciation

(The fixed assets are the long-term assets necessary to carry out the manufacturing of widgets)

Current assets:	Stocks	270	These are the raw materials and finished stock
Current assets:	Debtors	1,100	The amount owed by customers

(The current assets are short-term assets of the business that change day-to-day, depending on production / sales)

The total assets of the company are: 3,020

LIABILITIES OF THE BUSINESS

Bank loans:	Long term	750	Part-financing the fixed assets
Bank loans:	Overdraft	150	Financing day-to-day changes in current assets/current liabilities
Current liabilities:	Trade creditors	1,200	The amount owed to day-to-day suppliers
	Accrued taxes	210	PAYE & VAT due in normal way

The total liabilities of the company are: 2,310

Shareholders' funds = 710

(The shareholders' funds are the excess of total assets over total liabilities, that is, the net assets. It comprises the original amount invested by the shareholders as adjusted by subsequent accumulated profits or losses.)

A Simple Analysis of a Balance Sheet

- Long-term assets should be matched by long-term finance. The fixed assets in the widget manufacturing company total 1,650. Shareholders' funds are 710 and long-term loans 750, total 1,460. This shows a position of some financial strain in that the shortfall of 190 is financed by short-term creditors.

- Plant and machinery 790. The original cost was 2,630 seven years ago, depreciation written off 1,840 (70% of cost). This means that the plant and machinery is in the last third of its active life and replacement will be necessary in the foreseeable future. Replacement could mean difficulties in raising a loan because of strained finances and higher interest costs.

- Current assets total 1,370 and current liabilities (excluding bank overdraft) total 1,410. These assets/liabilities constantly change day-by-day and are reasonably in balance (though there may be a seasonal element). The bank overdraft of 150 should also be seen as a current liability. The short-term position shows some financial strain.

- Shareholders' funds at 710 are financing only 24% of the total assets of 3,020. Bank loans total 900, which, on one view, means that the bank has a higher amount in the business than the shareholders. Current thinking is that, in overall terms, bank loans/shareholders' funds should be no more than 50:50, though the finance of individual assets (such as premises) could have higher percentage borrowings.

- The balance sheet shows a 'tight' financial position. The ability to raise further bank loans is very restricted. A major factor is the looming replacement of the plant and machinery. A track record of sustained and good profitability over the next two-to-three years is critical to raising the necessary finance. An assessment of future maintainable profits will confirm or deny this possibility. A further investment by existing and or new shareholders (which may be hard to raise) will probably also prove necessary.

Chapter 4

The Multiple

The multiple should be based on a comparison with market and business sector sentiment as best can be identified at the time, and as adjusted for the individual circumstances of the company.

In pursuing his task of valuation, the valuer will consider the available comparisons and precedents. In Ireland, there will probably be few, if indeed any, comparable transactions available, particularly where the valuation of a small or medium-sized business is involved. Press reports about the purchase/sale of businesses tend to be short and simplistic in their analysis. There is no regular report or tabulated data in Ireland regarding such transactions, except occasional (usually annual) listings of mergers and acquisitions, which rarely include any data useful for valuation comparisons.

4–01

(See **para 4–11** regarding "The BDO Stoy Hayward Private Company Price Index", published in the UK.)

In valuing medium-to-large companies, comparisons with quoted companies are sometimes used (though, with so few quoted companies in Ireland, these may provide only outline comparisons). A valuer needs to be careful, in overall terms, that the comparison is reasonably like-to-like. The following comparisons between a private company and a quoted company should be taken into account in a private company valuation:

4–02

- P/Es (the 'price/earnings ratio': explained on page 41) of quoted companies are based on net-of-tax profits. The valuations of private companies are also based on net-of-tax profits.

- P/Es of quoted companies reflect the current purchase price of a small shareholding; a higher price (UK studies suggest

30% to 50% higher) would have to be paid for a large shareholding or to acquire the entire company.

- P/Es are based on the latest publicly available results and are therefore **historical**. The valuation of a private company shareholding is based on a multiple related to **future** earnings.

- Quoted company shares can be readily bought and sold; the same is not true for private company shareholdings. The difference is crucial and is summed up in one word: marketability.

- No two companies are identical, and simply being in the same business sector does not, in itself, mean that an unqualified comparison is valid. Businesses in the same business sector may sell quite different products and services.

- Quoted companies are generally far larger than private companies.

An informed valuer will recognise that what happens on the stockmarket cannot be seamlessly and unthinkingly translated to the valuation of private companies.

Price–Earnings Ratio

Commonly referred to as the *P/E ratio*, this is another term for a multiple of profits.

Example

A quoted company had pre-tax profits of €16,410,600 for the year ended 31 December 20xx and paid tax at 20% of those profits. Net-of-tax profits were therefore €13,128,480.

The company has 45 million ordinary shares issued. There are no other classes of issued shares. Earnings (i.e., net-of-tax profits) per ordinary share were therefore:

€13,128,480/45 million = €0.29 per share

The current market price of the company's share is €3.20, therefore the price-earnings ratio (P/E) is:

€3.20/€0.29 = P/E 11.0

In other words, the market values the company's shares at a multiple of 11.0 times net-of-tax profits.

The P/E is calculated on net-of-tax profits. Valuations of private companies are similarly calculated on net-of-tax profits.

Some companies may have different classes of issued ordinary shares and/or have granted share options on unissued shares. There may also be preference shares issued. Adjustments may therefore be necessary in calculating a P/E ratio.

Hindsight

4-03 Hindsight has no part in valuation. The *Holt v. IRC* case in the UK (1953) established that a valuer cannot use knowledge of subsequent events. The valuation must be based on the information (including general market circumstances, known as *'sentiment'*) available at the date of valuation. This is even where it is subsequently shown that such sentiment was misplaced, such as a later significant increase or decrease in market values.

Danckwerts J. in *Holt v. IRC* said:

> *"it is necessary to assume the prophetic vision of a prospective purchaser at the moment of the death of the deceased, and firmly to reject the wisdom which might be provided by the knowledge of subsequent events".*

4-04 Completing a valuation as of a date, say, five years ago means using the information in existence at or before that date. This is irrespective of what may subsequently have happened – for good or bad – to the company or generally in the marketplace. There have been numerous disputes regarding circumstances whereby a company was sold for a significantly higher or lower amount than a recent valuation or actual share transaction. The principle that hindsight has no part in valuation does not change in such circumstances. An attempt by the aggrieved party to allege negligence by the valuer or financial advisers is likely in such a case. A proper Letter of Engagement and good working papers will be the valuer's defence in these circumstances.

(See **Chapter 1**, The Role of the Valuer, and in particular, **para 1-05** on the legal duties and responsibilities of the valuer.)

4-05 Movements in market sentiment can greatly increase or decrease valuations, even though the circumstances of the company itself are largely unchanged. For example, in the 1980s, few medium-to-large companies sold for more than four or five times net-of-tax profits, reflecting general pessimism and uncertainty. Sentiment in the mid-to-late 1990s was the opposite: boom times in TMT stocks (technology, media and telecom) in particular, filtered down into sales of medium-to-large private companies in many sectors, almost irrespective of quality or prospects, at multiples of 10 to 15 times net-of-tax profits, and even higher on occasions. This slipped to a range of about six to 10 times net-of-tax profits by circa 2006 and the recent calamitous collapse in values, which started in late 2007 has continued into early 2010 (the time of writing).

What takes place at the highest levels of quoted companies in terms of multiples regarding acquisition/disposal/merger activity does filter down and influence valuations at lower levels. However, vendors, and sometimes valuers too, quite often believe that the higher levels of yesteryear are still applicable to some extent, any current downturn being temporary. The marketplace says otherwise. **4–06**

What history does show, sometimes in the most dramatic way, as occurred in the TMT sector (technology, media, and telecom) in the late 1990s, is that high valuations paradoxically lead to more purchases/sales of companies. However, history has repeatedly also shown that the drive to compete for acquisitions, or to participate in the latest venture capital or public offering becomes an end in itself, which, however, inevitably brings a downward (and usually sharp) correction in values to the apparent surprise of all except seasoned observers. This correction has happened three times in the last 40 years, in 1974, 1987 and 1999, not including the recent downturn in values (2007–2009) which has different origins. **4–07**

4-08   THE VALUATION OF BUSINESSES AND SHARES

Historic P/Es in Ireland

4-08 The charts of average P/Es on the Irish stockmarket below shows how multiples have varied, month by month, over the 20 years 1990 to 2009. The average daily P/Es in those years was as follows:

Average P/Es on the Irish Stockmarket, 1990–2009			
1990	11.86	2000	17.61
1991	12.38	2001	16.60
1992	12.62	2002	12.74
1993	14.93	2003	12.26
1994	14.89	2004	15.21
1995	12.51	2005	16.57
1996	12.51	2006	17.20
1997	16.17	2007	14.72
1998	20.49	2008	7.66
1999	18.98	2009	8.67

Source: Davy Stockbrokers

4-09 The average P/Es on the Irish stockmarket, whilst a useful guide to overall sentiment, have this drawback: the stockmarket was dominated by a small number of large stocks over the years (such as AIB, Bank of Ireland, CRH, with the additions of Ryanair and Tullow Oil, and the volatility of Elan).

4-10 Published comment suggests that, over the long term, P/Es in the main European and US stockmarkets have tended to gravitate to a *'mean'* P/E of circa 12, with good or bad times adjusting upwards and downwards on that figure. In contrast, the average Irish P/E for the 17 years 1990 to 2006 (excluding the collapse in values in the three years 2007 to 2009) was 15.03.

IRISH STOCKMARKET HISTORIC P/Es OVER 20 YEARS: 1990 TO 2009

	'90	'91	'92	'93	'94	'95	'96	'97	'98	'99	'00	'01	'02	'03	'04	'05	'06	'07	'08	'09
Jan	15.70	10.10	13.70	13.20	17.70	11.81	14.16	13.80	18.24	18.81	16.50	17.10	16.10	10.49	14.25	15.81	16.24	16.21	9.98	6.45
Feb	15.10	12.20	13.40	12.90	18.60	11.96	13.90	14.25	20.97	19.16	16.90	17.80	14.01	10.17	12.75	16.49	17.17	15.91	9.78	6.19
Mar	14.10	12.90	13.50	14.40	17.40	11.66	13.50	14.01	22.19	20.50	18.50	16.20	14.08	10.91	14.31	14.66	17.25	16.07	9.50	7.28
Apr	13.30	12.30	13.90	14.70	17.60	11.75	11.40	14.18	22.47	20.20	17.50	16.80	14.02	11.36	15.17	14.17	16.96	16.49	9.70	7.99
May	13.00	12.90	13.40	14.70	13.14	11.80	11.59	15.45	21.32	18.96	16.50	17.90	14.27	11.39	14.63	15.30	16.57	16.91	9.39	8.46
Jun	12.40	12.60	12.60	14.50	12.69	12.41	11.70	16.03	21.71	18.20	16.20	17.90	12.66	12.28	14.96	16.74	16.22	16.13	8.15	8.67
Jul	12.00	12.90	12.20	15.40	13.44	12.71	11.50	17.97	21.32	18.40	16.50	17.50	11.11	12.53	14.85	17.56	16.40	14.66	6.80	8.98
Aug	9.70	13.30	11.70	15.60	13.80	13.04	11.93	17.01	19.16	18.90	17.59	16.70	11.93	13.04	15.16	17.06	17.62	14.34	6.95	9.47
Sep	9.50	13.10	11.90	14.90	13.69	13.12	12.27	17.51	18.32	18.30	18.10	14.10	10.83	13.23	15.66	17.29	17.94	13.50	5.94	10.9
Oct	9.60	12.90	11.30	16.60	13.51	12.75	12.53	17.26	18.46	17.30	18.30	15.20	11.16	13.89	16.10	16.85	18.71	13.51	4.19	9.7
Nov	8.90	11.60	11.80	15.70	13.40	13.50	12.48	17.77	20.43	19.60	19.10	15.70	11.55	13.85	16.95	17.98	19.08	12.57	5.77	9.5
Dec	9.00	11.80	12.00	16.60	13.70	13.64	13.18	18.85	21.33	19.40	19.60	16.27	11.15	13.97	17.70	18.94	16.29	10.39	5.76	10.5
Average	11.86	12.38	12.62	14.93	14.89	12.51	12.51	16.17	20.49	18.98	17.61	16.60	12.74	12.26	15.21	16.57	17.20	14.72	7.66	8.67

Source: Davy Stockbrokers

4-10 THE VALUATION OF BUSINESSES AND SHARES

IRISH STOCKMARKET HISTORIC P/Es OVER 20 YEARS: 1990 TO 2009

The average P/E over the 17 years 1990 to 2006 was 15.03

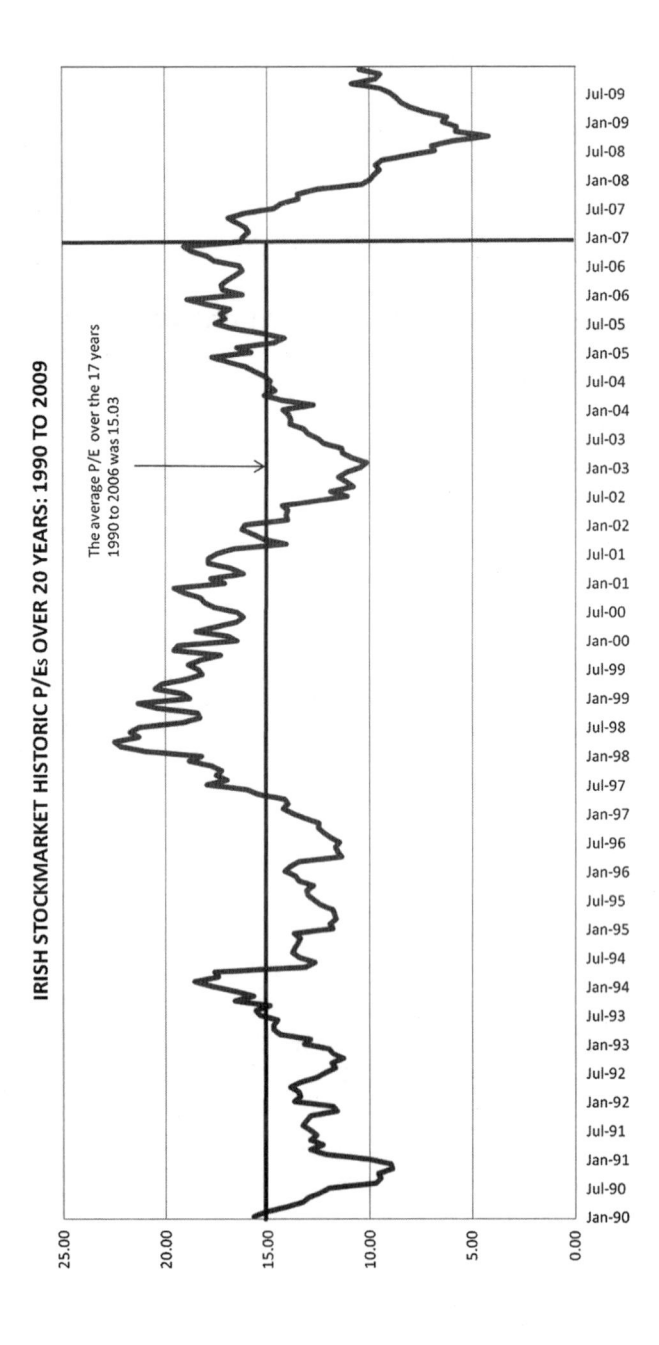

Historic P/Es in the United Kingdom

The *Financial Times* provides comprehensive P/Es on quoted individual companies and sectors. There is a range of indices available, as shown below. The current FTSE sector indices are on page 48. The number of quoted companies is in brackets.

FTSE ACTUARIES SHARE INDICES

Produced in conjunction with the Faculty and Institute of Actuaries

FTSE 100 (100)
FTSE 250 (250)
FTSE 250 ex Inv Co (203)
FTSE 350 (350)
FTSE 350 ex Inv Co (302)
FTSE 350 Higher Yield (97)
FTSE 350 Lower Yield (253)
FTSE SmallCap (265)
FTSE SmallCap ex Inv Co (163)
FTSE All-Share (615)
FTSE All-Share ex Inv Co (465)
FTSE All-Share ex Multinationals (552)
FTSE Fledgling (171)
FTSE Fledgling ex Inv Co (110)
FTSE All-Small (436)
FTSE All-Small ex Inv Co (273)
FTSE AIM All-Share (899)

Source: Financial Times. Further information is available on www.ftse.com.

FTSE Sector Indices

Oil & Gas (22)
Oil & Gas Producers (16)
Oil Equipment Services (6)

Basic Materials (28)
Chemicals (5)
Forestry & Papers (1)
Industrial Metals & Mining (3)
Mining (19)

Industrials (119)
Construction & Materials (11)
Aerospace & Defence (10)
General Industrials (7)
Electronic & Electrical Equipment (11)
Industrial Engineering (13)
Industrial Transportation (9)
Support Services (58)

Consumer Goods (37)
Automobile & Parts (1)
Beverages (4)
Food Producers (13)
Household Goods & Home Construction (11)
Leisure Goods (3)
Personal Goods (3)
Tobacco (2)

Healthcare (21)
Healthcare Equipment & Services (7)
Pharmaceuticals & Bio technology (14)

Telecommunications (8)
Fixed Line Telecommunications (6)
Mobile Telecommunications (2)

Utilities (9)
Electricity (3)
Gas Water & Multi-utilities (6)

Financials (246)
Banks (5)
Non-life Insurance (12)
Life Insurance/Assurance (9)
Real Estate Investment & Services (25)
Real Estate Investment Trusts (15)
Financial Services (30)
Equity Investment Instruments (150)

Non Financials (369)

Technology (32)
Software & Computer Services (23)
Technology Hardware & Equipment (9)

Consumer Service (93)
Food & Drug Retailers (6)
General Retailers (28)
Media (24)
Travel & Leisure (35)

Source: Financial Times

Overall P/Es as between particular business sectors can vary widely. This reflects market sentiment at the time for particular sectors. For example, in the UK, the mining sector is most times valued at lower than the overall 'norm', and healthcare higher than the 'norm'. Market sentiment in particular sectors can quickly react to perceived changes in national economic or sectoral circumstances; examples include the retail and construction sectors.

4–12

There is a useful comparison index regularly published in the UK, known as "The BDO Stoy Hayward Private Company Price Index" ("PCPI") (accessible on www.bdo.co.uk). Published quarterly, the PCPI tracks the relationship between non-financials P/Es published in the *Financial Times* and the P/Es of private company sales as per *'publicly available financial information on deals that complete in the quarter'.*

4–13

BDO also publishes an additional but similarly based index known as the "Private Equity Price Index" ("PEPI"), which tracks private equity transactions.

4–14

It is not possible to be specific at any one time as to interpreting the information in the BDO Indices but the indications are that over the long term the average P/E achieved on private company sales was circa 40%–45% less than the average quoted P/E.

4–15

(There are also the complications of making comparisons between the P/Es of private and quoted companies to consider. See para **4–02**.)

Revenue Valuations

The Revenue Commissioners, in assessing capital taxes, have an interest in the valuation of shares. An extract from the Revenue guidelines from their Capital Tax Acquisitions Tax Manual is shown below. (The complete guidelines, dated 22 September 2009, are in **Appendix Four.**)

4–16

Note that the Revenue guidelines quote a discount of 20% to stockmarket P/Es for the valuation of private companies. This 20% is comparable, in that it is calculated on the same basis, to the BDO discount of 40%–45% mentioned at **para 4–13**.

It should always be clearly understood in valuation practice that shareholdings in private companies cannot be seen as an alternative to an investment in shares quoted on the stockmarket.

4–17

Extract From Revenue Guidelines on Share Valuations

Valuation of Shares

Valuation is not an exact science. The value of a shareholding depends on many factors – the nature/size of the shareholding passing, profitability of the business and its future prospects in the marketplace at the time of the transaction.

When valuing shares in unquoted companies for tax purposes, the shares passing must be valued on the basis of a hypothetical sale in a hypothetical open market between a hypothetical willing vendor and a hypothetical willing purchaser.

Depending on the nature of the company's business, different valuation methodologies may be employed.

Valuation Based on Earnings

Trading and manufacturing companies are normally valued on the basis of a multiple of their maintainable after-tax profits. This multiple is known as the price earnings ratio. The multiple used may vary depending on the particular industry in which the company is engaged.

The appropriate multiple is normally selected by reference to a quoted company/companies in the same industry. Financial information in respect of quoted companies is published regularly in the national newspapers. The results of these companies are analysed in relation to their trading performance and the prices at which their shares are sold are expressed as a multiple of their after-tax profits.

When a suitable quoted company has been identified, the normal practice is to use the multiple of after-tax profits appropriate to that quoted company, less a discount of 20% to compensate for the lack of access to the market which a quote on the stock exchange provides, i.e.

If the multiple of after-tax profits for the quoted company is 10, the appropriate multiple for an unquoted company would be 8, but this may be further reduced if the unquoted company is a relatively small one.

This is known as the earnings method of valuation and most companies are valued on this basis.

If a company has retained profits or assets of any sort not immediately required for the purpose of its trade, the value of all such assets would normally be added to the company's earnings value.

Risk

The varying overall P/Es between sectors is general confirmation that a share price reflects a multiple of future maintainable profits as adjusted for risk. For example, mining is relatively unstable and healthcare is relatively stable, and investors are willing to pay a higher price for that stability.

4–18

There are other aspects to understanding the use of a multiple in valuations. Investment in shares in a company carries significant risk, particularly in private companies. Small-to-medium-sized businesses do not have the capacity to carry bad times, their customer base is limited, banks are restrictive on loans, and the small scale in itself allows easy entry into the same business by competitors. The multiple for a small-to-medium-sized business will be less than for larger businesses.

4–19

The larger the business, the easier it is to value/sell. A medium-to-large business can employ management independent of the owners, offers more security to weather bad times and its investment in plant and machinery, working capital, etc., is funded more easily by the banks. The market for a potential sale of the business will be wider.

4–20

Suggested Multiples

4-21 Suggested multiples for the sale of entire businesses (as at early 2010) may be stated as follows:

Size of Business	Net-of-tax Maintainable Profits	Suggested multiple
Large	€15 million and higher	6 to 8
Medium-to-large	€10 million to €15 million	5 to 6
Medium	€5 million to €10 million	4 to 6
Small-to-medium	€1 million to €5 million	3 to 6
Small	Less than €1 million	2 to 4
Very small	(See **Chapter 9**, Valuing a Small Business)	—

4-22 The suggested multiples are based on the following assumptions:

- 100% of the company is being sold/valued.

- It can reasonably be demonstrated that a quoted Irish P/E comparison, either in approximately the same business sector or in the overall market (as adjusted for any obvious anomalies) would be 12 or better.

- If the foregoing P/E is lower than 12, the suggested multiples would be adjusted proportionately downwards. If more than 12, no adjustment upwards. In other words, the multiples as shown are maximum, unless there are exceptional circumstances.

- Due adjustment, based on the judgement of the valuer, should be made for higher than normal borrowings or surplus assets in the company.

EBITDA

It was popular in the 1990s, in the valuation of large companies or in comparing the performances of companies, to refer to EBITDA. This stood for earnings before interest, tax, depreciation and amortisation.

It was thought that EBITDA stripped out the distortions caused by different policies on depreciation, different tax regimes (meaning international companies), and the fact that some companies used borrowings more than others, and so on.

The idea was to get to the core profitability of the business and allow like-to-like comparisons between companies in the same sector, including international companies. After an initial flurry of interest and the term EBITDA being used with abandon as the new way forward in valuations (earnings valuations being so old-fashioned), it became discredited as a method of valuation because in itself it was fundamentally flawed; an example being that a heavily borrowed company was treated as being equal to a company that had little or no borrowings. Similarly, a company with depreciation on relatively non-productive assets was treated the same as a similar company with depreciation on highly productive assets.

The 'death' of EBITDA came when Warren Buffett, the legendary investor, suggested its use was effectively *'fraudulent'*. Some financial press commentators and investment bankers still do not know that EBITDA is dead.

Chapter 5

The Minority Position

The most vexed question in valuations is the position of a minority shareholder.

5-01 **Chapter 2,** Fundamentals of Valuation (**paras 2–19 to 2–24**), explains the position of the minority shareholder.

5-02 It is accepted practice to value a minority shareholding by reference to the value of the entire company, and apply the appropriate discount as follows:

(These discounts have emerged over many years through accepted valuation practice and published Revenue guidelines on valuation.)

Shareholding	Discount*
75% and higher	No discount but sometimes 5% if less than 80%
50% + one share and higher	10% to 15%
50%	20% to 30%
25% + one share and higher	35% to 40%
25% and less	50% to 70%

It is important to note that the spread of shareholdings may be a factor in deciding on the appropriate discount. See **para 2–23**.

(*See **paras 6–10 to 6–18** re valuations based on the net assets of non-trading (such as property or investment) companies.)

Dividend-based Valuations

For many years, accepted valuation was that minority shareholdings were valued on a dividend yield basis, meaning a multiple of the dividend being paid. It was, on occasion, the practice to value on the basis of what dividend could be paid, even if none was paid.

5-03

The dividends valuation model is still, strictly speaking, the foremost method of valuation for minority shareholdings. However, changes in the financial world, as explained below, have changed the focus to valuations based on profits not just for a majority shareholding but also for a minority shareholding.

5-04

Only established, large private companies, usually owned by second or third generation shareholders with family origins, actually pay regular dividends. Such companies are now few in number due to the difficulties of continuing a business into successive generations.

5-05

Apart from small-to-medium-sized proprietor-owned companies, the emphasis in shareholder investment, since the early 1990s, is generally on seeking capital growth, meaning retaining all profits to finance future growth. In any event, the shareholders may not wish to receive dividends because of higher personal taxes compared to (eventual) lower taxed capital gains.

5-06

The availability of larger bank borrowings to companies in recent years has also mitigated against dividends, the available profits being first used to service such borrowings. The larger capital base for investment through borrowings, in theory, means greater investment for greater return to shareholders in the long run.

5-07

Comparisons of dividends in quoted companies has its drawbacks, not least because many newer quoted companies, including large companies (such as Ryanair at time of writing), have a policy of not paying dividends, instead seeking to reward their shareholders through capital appreciation in an increased share price. While a directly comparable company is unlikely to be

5-08

found, it may be possible to find a sector comparison (though probably in the London rather than the Dublin stockmarket) or, more likely, a general overall dividend yield for the entire market.

5–09   For example, the Irish stockmarket may have an overall dividend yield of, say, 2%, meaning that an investment of €100 in the total market would yield annual dividends of €2. This, however, is distorted by the some companies not paying dividends.

5–10   It is established valuation practice to increase the dividend yield of quoted companies when valuing minority shareholdings in private companies for, *inter alia,* the following reasons (a higher yield means a lower valuation):

- The continuity of dividends in private companies, unlike quoted companies, is not designed to maintain a share price or to maintain an attractive market in the shares.

- A private company does not have access to public capital markets (new share issues, rights issues, loan stocks of all kinds) and its main source of finance for new or replacement investment is likely to be retained profits, with the consequent restriction, or lack of orderly continuity, on dividends.

- A private company, under company law, restricts the right of shareholders to freely transfer its shares. Consequently, there is not an open market in those shares.

5–11   For the foregoing reasons, accepted valuation practice suggests that where a private company has a good profits record and is paying a realistic dividend, the dividend yield on the quoted company or quoted sector, used as a comparison, is increased by between one-half to one-third, depending on the perception of risk attaching to the continuity of the dividend and to the shareholding. Some valuers argue that the yield should automatically be doubled, unless the private company is exceptionally stable and profitable.

5–12   An example will illustrate that an increased dividend yield means a lower value:

EXAMPLE

An annual dividend of €10,000 is paid by a private company to a minority shareholder. It is noted that if it were a quoted company the dividend yield would be 5%, i.e., the shareholding would have a value of €200,000 (€200,000 @ 5% = €10,000).

For the reasons mentioned, in making the valuation of the private company shareholding, the valuer decided it was appropriate to increase the dividend yield by one-half, to 7.5%.

A dividend yield of 7.5% would mean a valuation of €133,333 for the private company shareholding (€133,333 @ 7.5% = €10,000).

No New Thinking

Despite the sophistication of *'financial engineering'*, many changes and additions in company law, and the investment emphasis on capital growth (and dividends somehow being designated as old-fashioned), no new thinking or new market practice has emerged regarding the vexed question of minority discount.

A minority shareholder, properly advised, in selling-out may sometimes be able to negotiate what is referred to as an *'embarrassment clause'* whereby, if the purchaser (usually being the majority shareholder in this context) sells out the entire company within a stated period (perhaps one or two years) after the purchase, the minority shareholder receives (say) 50% of any resultant profit on the shareholding in additional consideration.

> **CASE HISTORY: DOWNTURN IN PROFITS**
>
> An established textiles business depended on manufacturing 'own brand label' clothing (for two major retail chains) for about 45% of its total sales. The own brand business was competitive insofar as it was subject to a tendering three-year cycle. The business was owned as to 60%:40% by two families, one of which (60%) had similar textile interests elsewhere. The business was well-managed and reasonably profitable.
>
> The company lost one of the contracts, on tender, comprising approx 26% of its total sales. It was a hard blow, involving redundancies and cost-saving measures, and the company's future survival was in some, though not immediate, doubt. There was also a question of significant re-equipment/investment in the foreseeable future, and the viability of this investment at a time of uncertainty.
>
> The 60% shareholders offered to 'rescue' the business by buying out the 40% shareholders, and amalgamating it with its other textile interests. Disagreement on price subsequently ensued and the price was referred to an expert valuer, binding on both parties.
>
> The expert valued the business on the basis of: (a) future maintainable net-of-tax profits at 55% of the profits in the financial year immediately prior to the loss of the contract; (b) deducting from (a), a calculated additional future depreciation and interest costs regarding the re-equipment/investment; (c) applying a low multiple of four to reflect uncertainty; (d) adding a premium of 20% to reflect the *'special purchaser'* element, i.e. the purchaser would benefit from elimination of duplicated costs, synergy; and (e) not applying a minority discount on the basis that the two families had a history of quasi-partnership in the business.

Chapter 6

The Role of Assets

An important principle of valuation is what is known as 'the unit of valuation principle', that is, the business should be valued as a totality and not as the sum of individual values.

Any business has a mix of tangible assets and management/ employees, supplemented by a range of intangibles such as market knowledge, intellectual property, expertise of all kinds, and so on.   6-01

The notion that the net assets in themselves in some way represent a valuation of the business has no basis in theory or in fact. The value of a business derives from its ability to earn profits.   6-02

(Note the exception that passive (i.e. non-trading) property and investment companies would be valued on a net assets basis. See **paras 6-10 to 6-18**.)

The earnings valuation of a business arrived at on the basis of expected future maintainable profits, capitalised at an appropriate multiple, may bear little relationship to the value of the underlying net assets on the balance sheet. Net assets are defined as the gross assets less the gross liabilities. The net assets are the same figure as the *'shareholders' funds'* on the balance sheet. It may be necessary to substitute an independent property valuation and/or the market value for any investments to calculate an updated net assets value.   6-03

It could reasonably be argued that, in the case of a continuing business, assets are worth no more than they will earn. A buyer may be willing to pay a premium on the value of the underlying net assets if the future maintainable profits are there to justify it. On the other hand, in the absence of special   6-04 circumstances, if the profits are not there, it does not make sense to pay the value of the net assets. It is the right to receive future income that is being purchased.

6-05 It may be said, where there is poor profitability or losses, that a purchaser could make better use of the net assets and/or that the net assets could be realised and used for other purposes. This could have some validity in limited circumstances. A valuer needs to be careful, however, that he is not in fact including the incoming expertise of the potential purchaser as being part of the valuation.

(See **para 3-07** regarding the expertise of the purchaser.)

6-06 The history of assets being influential in past valuations may explain why it is sometimes referred to as a rival or complementary method of valuation to the multiple of profits method (an earnings valuation). The net assets approach to valuation still occasionally surfaces as commentary in the financial press. Prior to the early 1990s, it was common valuation practice, for the value of net assets to be seen as a cap on earnings valuations. Potential purchasers would seek to see the purchase price underpinned by net assets representing at least 60% to 70% of the purchase price.

> **EXAMPLE**
>
> The valuation based on a multiple of profits was €2.4 million. The net assets were €1.4 million. The valuation was therefore capped at €2.0 million, the net assets then representing 70% of that amount.

6-07 The net assets approach to valuation is now viewed by experienced practitioners as obsolete. The principal reason for this is the enormous growth in expertise-led, and not asset-based, companies. Examples include businesses engaged in software development, financial services, entertainment, advertising, recruitment, information technology, and so on.

When Net Assets are Relevant

A valuer should review the net assets of the company in carrying out a valuation with reference to two particular aspects which, on occasion, can materially affect a valuation, namely: **6–08**

- A close look at the nature and age of the fixed assets of the business (plant, machinery, equipment), can show a near requirement for replacement with consequent higher depreciation and finance charges, and thereby lower future maintainable profits.
- Surplus assets should be added to the valuation based on future maintainable profits. Examples of this would be cash balances, investments, unused properties, not needed for the operation of the business.

There is an apparent contradiction, involving the role of net assets in valuation, where in a theoretical situation two otherwise identical businesses, valued on the same multiple of future maintainable profits, have differing net assets. This perhaps illustrates that many valuations will have some element of subjective judgement best addressed by the experience of the valuer. **6–09**

(See the case history on page 62.)

As explained above, the net assets alone should not be used to determine the value of a company, unless the assets have readily realisable values, such as in passive property- and investment-owning companies. These are not trading enterprises. **6–10**

A majority interest in such a company is valued on the basis of net assets (using up-to-date valuations on the underlying properties and/or investments). A minority interest has no access to the net assets nor is it in a position to dictate the use of the net assets. It would be a different situation if a minority interest were such that it conferred control or effective control when grouped with one or more other minority shareholdings. In such an event, the valuation of a minority shareholding may be based on the pro-rata net assets value. **6–11**

(See **para 6–13** below on minority discount in this regard.)

Case History: A Valuation with Strong Assets

A distribution/retail business, in second generation family ownership, had lacklustre profits but its properties had become increasingly valuable. A family member, not an employee or director, wished to sell his 17% shareholding to fund a marital separation settlement. The remaining shareholdings were held 32%:31%:20%, the two largest being employee/directors, and who were willing to jointly purchase the 17% shareholding if agreement could be reached on the price.

The net assets of the company, following revaluations of the properties, totalled €11.1 million. One property, valued at €3.5 million had become valuable because of its prime location and could be replaced elsewhere by a rented property at approx €120,000/€140,000 per year.

The business was valued on behalf of the prospective purchasers at €1.260 million net-of-tax profits × 6.5 times = €8.190 million and a minority discount of 35%. A valuer for the prospective seller argued for the net asset value of €11.1 million and no minority discount because of the strength of the assets.

The compromise was a price of €1,433,440 for the 17% shareholding, calculated as follows:

Net-of-tax profits €1.140 million × 6.5 times (i.e. after deducting €120,000 for rent adjustment)	= €7.410 million
Add: net realisable value of surplus property (i.e. after expenses and capital gains tax)	= €3.000 million
	€10.410 million
€10.410 million × 17% = €1,769,700 less 20% minority discount	€1,415,760

THE ROLE OF ASSETS

6-12 Passive property- and investment-owning companies in the long run tend to pay dividends to shareholders (usually after borrowings have been paid off or largely paid off), on the basis that such companies are really investment managers for the underlying owners, the shareholders.

6-13 A minority shareholding in such companies can normally be valued on a dividend yield basis. In circumstances of a significant minority shareholding (defined as perhaps 20% or higher) and no single majority shareholding, a valuation pro-rata to the underlying net assets may be more appropriate. Minority discount would likely still apply but at a lesser level (perhaps half) than applicable in an earnings valuation.

(See **para 5-02** for a schedule of minority discount.)

6-14 Sometimes the transfer of a business may be undertaken on the basis that the purchaser acquires the assets of the business, meaning only the fixed assets of, say, a factory premises, plant and machinery, equipment, etc. There may also be a commitment to acquire stocks at an agreed value and/or to provide continued employment to some or all of the workforce. This often arises in receiverships or liquidations.

6-15 There is no particular formula of valuation that can be followed in such circumstances. The vendor, usually a receiver or liquidator, will hope to achieve a higher amount than would be achieved by piecemeal realisation of assets and there may also be a saving on redundancy costs. The purchaser seeks to pay as little as possible but, presumably, will have done some homework on valuation based on the expected future maintainable profits from the acquisition of the equivalent of a going concern but without the related liabilities.

6-16 A question that invariably arises in the valuation of a passive property or investment-owning company is whether realisation costs (including any taxation clawbacks for capital allowances and/or capital gains tax) should be taken into account in calculating net asset values. There are several issues involved here, including:

- Capital gains tax can be incurred twice: once on the realisation of the property or investment within the company; and again if the company is liquidated, the shareholders being liable to capital gains tax on the resultant distribution. Capital gains tax and any taxation clawbacks are only taken into account once in the potential realisation of assets within the company.

- The capital gains tax that may be paid on realisation by a shareholder is an individual matter, and is not relevant to a net assets valuation of the underlying shareholding.

- Estimated realisation costs (such as legal fees and estate agent costs) should be taken into account in the calculation of net assets. These costs would usually be approximately 1% for marketable investments and in the range of 2% to 5% for properties and more complex investments.

6–17 It is common to find that *'knock-on'* valuations are involved insofar as the passive property or investment-owning company in turn holds shareholdings in other private companies. A valuer needs to make a careful assessment of the tax position on realisations in such circumstances.

6–18 It is the experience of the author that (in the long term) the lack of realisation in the value of shareholdings in passive property and investment-owning companies causes more legal actions for oppression of minority than in any other type of company. This often happens where the shareholdings have devolved to one or two new generations of family owners.

Intellectual Property

6–19 The valuation of businesses, the primary assets of which comprise the development and/or ownership of intellectual property, provides particular challenges to the valuer. (See **Chapter 16, Intellectual Property**.)

High Net Assets

6–20 There is a view that high net assets backing to an earnings valuation reduces risk and that the valuation deserves to be increased accordingly. There is some validity to this view for the following reasons:

- It will likely be easier for the business itself to obtain bank finance, as the net assets may provide security for such finance.

- There may be the possibility that, should the business falter as a trading enterprise, the underlying assets could be realised or put to alternative better use.

Whether or not this factor should be taken into account will be a matter for the judgement of the valuer in the individual circumstances.

Goodwill as an Asset

In the context of an owner intending to sell his business, goodwill will be mentioned by the owner as being an asset of the business. The owner will probably see goodwill as representing the hard work and risk taken to bring the business to what it is and, accordingly, in the owner's mind a purchaser should pay (handsomely) for this goodwill.   **6-21**

The reality is, however, is that a potential purchaser of a business is only interested in the future maintainable profits and has no knowledge or interest in what has gone before except to the extent that it may impinge, for good or bad, on his future ownership of the business.   **6-22**

The question of goodwill being an asset of the business comes back to *'the unit of valuation'* principle mentioned at the outset of this chapter. This is further explained below.   **6-23**

The term *'goodwill'* is an accountant's nightmare. Most people in business probably understand roughly what it means, but even many accountants and bankers are at a loss when trying to explain goodwill and its relevance, if any, in the context of valuation. In some circumstances, accounting for goodwill can lead to absurdities as explained below.   **6-24**

To add to the confusion, *'goodwill'* is a term or word having different meanings in different contexts. It is intangible, difficult to explain and is frequently misunderstood. In the context of valuation, goodwill can be no less mysterious, but in reality now has little, if any, relevance.   **6-25**

The nearest we have to a basic definition of business goodwill is probably that of Lord Eldon in *Crutwell v. Lye* in 1810:   **6-26**

> "... nothing more than the probability that the old customers will resort to the old place even though the old trader or shopkeeper has gone."

A later variation (1901), though similar, is Lord McNaughten's definition in *IRC v. Muller*:

> "... the benefit of the good name, reputation and connection of a business. It is the attractive force which brings in custom."

6-27 In accounting terms, following an acquisition, the difference between the value of the net assets and the purchase price is described as goodwill in the books (as an asset on the balance sheet) of the acquiring company. Occasionally, there is negative goodwill where the net assets are greater than the purchase price. Accounting standards require that goodwill is written off in a particular way, which as such has no bearing on valuation (except that any write-off of goodwill is added back in ascertaining future maintainable profits).

6-28 The point of the foregoing is to demonstrate that the accounting definition of goodwill, as above, can be an unintentional absurdity. This is perhaps best explained by pointing out that service companies (such as advertising agencies or recruitment companies) tend to have a much lower percentage of net assets to purchase price than a manufacturing concern. Paradoxically, service companies have higher valuations of goodwill than manufacturing companies, which is absurd. This is even more so when it is considered that the goodwill of service companies is frequently vested in the expertise of key personnel, susceptible to departure, rather than in the ownership of a manufactured product.

6-29 The particular feature of goodwill, as generally understood to attach to a name, a product or a service, is that, although it can be used or transferred, this must be on the basis of the business as a whole. Other assets, however, may be sold separately, even if only at their break-up value. If, on occasion, goodwill is sold separately (such as a company or trade name that denotes quality or tradition capable of exploitation by the acquiring business) it could only be on the assumption that the purchaser would itself provide the other assets necessary to continue the business relating to the goodwill.

In this latter regard, the valuation of goodwill is not unlike the debate about including the valuation of a brand as an asset on the balance sheet. A brand is a form of goodwill.

The debate about goodwill and its valuation has continued over many years. The term 'goodwill' is still there but its usage and valuation is now seen differently. It is accepted in valuation practice that goodwill is not in itself an asset but that it arises (for accounting reasons) because investors, together with management, assemble a range of assets into a business generating profits which, when capitalised at the appropriate multiple, values the entire entity in excess of the underlying net assets, thus pursuing the argument that, if the proper return on investment (profits) is not there, there is no goodwill. If it is there, the *'premium'* over the net assets reflects its existence.

Case History: The Influence of Assets on Valuation

This is best illustrated by an exam-type question. There are two identical companies, A and B, both in the distribution business, each making €2.5 million future maintainable net-of-tax profits per year.

Company A owns its own premises valued at €3.0 million and Company B rents its premises at €200,000 per year.

Requirement

As both companies are making the same pre-tax profits, and accepting that the basis of valuation is normally a multiple thereof, do you believe the companies should have the same valuation and if not, why not? Give reasons for your answer.

Answer

Companies A and B should be valued on the same multiple. However, for comparability, the pre-tax profits of Company A should be reduced by €200,000 (the equivalent rent) to €2.3 million, and the value of the premises added to the valuation:

	Company A	Company B
Net-of-tax profits (adjusted for rent)	€2.3 million	€2.5 million
Multiple (say) × 8	€18.4 million	€20.0 million
Add value of premises	€3.0 million	-
Total valuation	€21.4 million	€20.0 million

The difference between the two valuations is due to a higher multiple being applied to the rental for the property than to the net-of-tax profits. It would be reasonable to expect that an even higher price than €21.4 million (obtained through negotiation) would be paid for Company A, to reflect the security provided by the premises.

Chapter 7

Rules of Thumb

A potential purchaser should be wary of a valuation based on a 'rule of thumb' approach.

Commentators, financial analysts, estate agents, and others, often like to believe, or at least promulgate the belief, that the valuation of a business in a particular sector can be stated as some simple formula such as *'x times turnover'*, a percentage of something, or a multiple per unit, that unit being a hotel room, a subscriber, and so on. Sometimes, advisers charge extraordinary fees for imparting such wisdom in an apparently knowledgeable manner. This wisdom is known collectively as *'rules of thumb'*. — 7–01

Common sense dictates that the reason for acquiring a business, or an interest in a business, is to obtain an economic return, meaning future profits and/or capital appreciation. However, the use of *'rules of thumb'* in valuing a business is at best arbitrary, is not based on economic assessment, and carries little if any logic beyond being some kind of shorthand valuation usually put about within the business sector itself. — 7–02

Sometimes particular sectors seem to have 'rules of thumb' for valuation. A spate of acquisitions in a particular sector (such as pharmacies, regional newspapers, undertakers, recruitment agencies, etc.) is seen as a pattern that can be reduced to a common factor such as a multiple of turnover, a price per underlying unit, a percentage of funds under management, and similar. Industry and trade associations, with members always anxious to know the value of their businesses, sometimes publish such *'norms'* in trade newsletters and journals. Financial press commentators too can create a 'norm' by simply relating the sale price of a particular business to some underlying statistic in the business, such as the price being X times the turnover, the number of subscribers divided into the price, the price expressed — 7–03

7-04 THE VALUATION OF BUSINESSES AND SHARES

as a percentage of the amount of funds under management. This 'norm', having been published and thereby accorded a status, is then perceived as a comparison or benchmark for any future transactions in the same sector, even where it bears little relation to the reality of the marketplace.

> In Ireland, there are insufficient transactions to identify and maintain any *'rules of thumb'*, with the exception of licensed premises (pubs). This has not, however, prevented anecdotal evidence being 'knowledgeably' quoted from time-to-time.
>
> Much of what is attested as 'norms' in Ireland seems to have been taken from the UK trade press. Sectors such as convenience stores are quoted as valued at so many weeks turnover, insurance brokerages valued by annual commissions, and so on.

7-04 The underlying premise to a 'rule of thumb' basis of valuation, if there can be a premise at all, has to be a belief that profitability in the sector does not vary greatly, and that therefore almost any company in the sector will have the same characteristics. This is obviously irrational because the following factors may differ:

- Rented versus owned premises
- Different levels of borrowings
- Young versus mature businesses
- Use of technology
- New versus old equipment
- Age and experience profiles of key employees

7-05 A 'norm' is an average. An average by definition includes high and low and does not distinguish between a good and a bad business. An average is not excused by saying it relates to a typical business. A business may be described as typical only insofar as it has, for example, a turnover similar to other businesses in the same sector. However, one or two common characteristics do not negate the differences between businesses as set out at **para 7-04** above.

7-06 A potential purchaser should be wary of a valuation based on a 'rule of thumb' approach. Examples abound of unwise acquisitions made through following such an approach, sometimes referred to as *'formula purchases'*.

7-07 An example in this regard was the UK and US mania in the 1990s among companies in the financial sector buying fund management companies based on a percentage of funds under management. It started off at about 1.5%, escalated and even reached 5% in some cases. This could make some sense if quality, size, fees, were the same. Purchasers quickly found out this was not the case; most paid too much and some incurred substantial losses in sorting out their expensive acquisitions.

7-08 Similar stories, in the UK, can be related regarding 'formula purchases' of undertakers, hotels, pubs and restaurant chains, recruitment agencies, insurance brokerages, advertising agencies, estate agents, newspapers, pharmacies, and even nursing homes. A high proportion of these acquisitions subsequently unravelled. It was mainly *'people businesses'* (such as estate, advertising and recruitment agencies) that lost the most money for their new owners.

7-09 The heaviest personal losses in the stockmarket incurred through unwise purchases/investments were during the 2000 boom in technology-related shares, with fledgling companies being priced at multiples of turnover (in public offerings as well as acquisitions), such turnover frequently being aspirational rather than factual.

7-10 It can be the case, however unscientific, that certain valuations are based and/or accepted on something akin to 'rules of thumb'. For example, the Revenue work manual (22 September 2009) on the valuation of shares regarding Capital Acquisitions Tax states the following:

> *"Companies which own or operate Licensed Premises or Restaurants or whose business is in the services sector, such as Insurance Brokers, Quantity Surveyors, Architectural Practices, Consulting Engineers, Legal etc. are normally valued on the basis of a multiple of their turnover, fees or commissions."*

7-11 A variation on the 'rule of thumb' basis of valuation, though not described as such, is the established practice by estate agents of valuing licensed premises (pubs) by the application of a multiple to turnover. Hotels too are often valued on a similar basis.

7-12 The underlying premise here seems to be that a pub or a hotel is a property which comprises a business. This, in theory, provides some undefined form of stability and security through the property itself, the usage in terms of the turnover generated within the property in turn then defining the price of the property/business.

7-13 It is an unsatisfactory method of valuation. There are all the variations of size, mix of sales (drink, food, entertainment, bedrooms), the location (city, suburban, rural), size of site, owners' accommodation or not, car parking, state of repair. Nevertheless, the market, in terms of potential purchasers and lending banks, appears willing to accept turnover-based valuations.

7-14 In summary, relying on a 'rule of thumb' as a basis for valuation is flawed. If a 'rule of thumb' is to have any use at all, it can be no more than a preliminary indication as to a seller's expectation of price. This expectation has to be met by the reality that a valuation is about market value, not a pre-ordained 'norm'. A potential purchaser, properly advised, will not buy on a 'rule of thumb' valuation.

Chapter 8

Grievance is not a Method of Valuation

As any experienced valuation practitioner will testify, it is difficult to handle grievance valuations.

In the experience of the author, most valuations of shares and businesses arise from a perceived grievance: the *'angry'* valuation. It is not always appreciated by an aggrieved party instructing the valuer that the valuation is not intended to be a measurement of his grievance, unless the matter complained of has led to a diminution in the value of his shareholding. Common grievances, in the context of share valuation, include: 8–01

- The company is doing particularly well and minority shareholders feel they should share in this prosperity, particularly where the company is perceived as having become valuable in a rising market for the sale of such companies. The pressure is usually for some or all of the smaller shareholdings to be purchased, possibly by the company itself.

- A founding shareholder, who is perhaps also a director/employee, falls out with his co-directors over respective roles and rewards and/or performances within the company.

- Shareholdings in an established business have devolved to a new generation, one or more of whom are denied the previous benefits attaching to the shareholding, such as a directorship or employment, and particularly in circumstances where other shareholders are perceived as receiving such benefits.

- The proper legal paperwork as regards shareholdings was never completed and there are differing views as to the correct ownership of shareholdings in the company. This type of dispute is surprisingly common.

- Fellow shareholders, or family members as shareholders, grow to hate each other and find a reason to fallout.

- The owner of the business wishes to sell out, for retirement or other reasons, and requests a valuation based on the money he wants rather than on the actual value of the business. It is often difficult for an owner to accept that what may represent many years of hard work and difficulties overcome, in itself, is of no interest or value to a potential purchaser.

- Family businesses are often akin to *'lifestyle'* businesses, that is, businesses that provide benefits to director/employee shareholders, whether that is the ability to employ children and other relatives at will, charge entertainment and sponsorship costs of a personal nature to the company, access to/or usage of wider business and social connections, and similar benefits. The independent valuation of a shareholding in such circumstances, as instructed by an outgoing or non-participant shareholder, will likely be rejected by the aggrieved shareholder as not representing *'the true value'*.

- Lawyers acting in marital separation for a spouse (the spouse usually not being a shareholder), may sometimes encourage a valuer to put an unrealistically high valuation on the other spouse's shareholding in a business, in order that the non-participant spouse can acquire a large lump sum and/or other assets as a *'quid pro quo'*. Experienced valuation practitioners will resist such encouragement.

The Response to a Grievance

8-02 The approach to valuation, in circumstances of an aggrieved shareholder, is no different to any other valuation, except that it may be prudent to value a shareholding in the normal way (usually meaning a minority discount) and to also show a second valuation based on the proportion of the shareholding, without discount, to the company as a whole. A valuer should insist on specific written instructions, confirming that the grievance has no relevance to the valuation. The instructions will usually come from a solicitor acting on behalf of the aggrieved shareholder. Ambiguity as to the relevance of the grievance to the valuation can involve the valuer in subsequent protracted and difficult correspondences.

8-03 Any experienced valuation practitioner will testify that it can be difficult to handle grievance valuations. The legal advisers are there to assist in the situation but the grievance is invariably centred on money. One party wants a huge pay-out via the valuation and the responding party does not want to pay at all. *'Hired gun'* type valuations by some valuers make this situation worse.

8-04 One or both parties will likely be difficult personalities, rational thought and reasonable behaviour being remote in the circumstances. Integrity, meaning objectivity, independence and impartiality, is the hallmark of the professional valuer. This can be difficult to explain in circumstances where the instructing party is attempting to dictate the amount of the valuation, which is often the case.

8-05 The alleged grievance can spill over into compensation demands that should (in the eyes of the instructing party) be included in the valuation, or *'vice versa'* from the other side. The demand is that the valuation should be pitched at a higher or lower level than is normally justified, as some form of punishment/compensation for the alleged grievance.

8-06 To add to the above pressure on the valuer, it is common for an aggrieved shareholder to search everywhere and produce a press cutting, or 'bar stool evidence', which confirms to him that huge profitability for the business has been suppressed or is in sight and/or that his shareholding should be valued at some great multiple or other based on a press report.

8-07 A major difficulty experienced by a valuer in a *'grievance'* valuation, when acting for the aggrieved party, is obtaining adequate information. Often, only the audited accounts will be grudgingly provided, the directors not being prepared to offer any other information. This will commonly result in legal correspondences and/or proceedings to obtain the information.

8-08 A useful overall definition of the necessary information in such circumstances is provided by the Taxes Consolidation Act 1997 (section 548(4)), as follows (in the context of determining the open market value of an asset for the purpose of taxation):

> *"...all the information which a prudent prospective purchaser of the asset might reasonably require if such*

prospective purchaser were proposing to purchase it from a willing vendor by private treaty and at arms' length".

8-09　　In these difficult circumstances while trying to obtain the necessary information for a valuation, it may be helpful for a valuer to offer to sign a *'Letter of Confidentiality'* concerning any information provided. This letter would usually confirm that the information will not be disclosed to any third party and/or will be returned without keeping a copy and/or be destroyed after any resultant transaction. The solicitors for the parties should be able to agree the contents of such a letter.

CASE HISTORY: 50:50 SHAREHOLDERS

An established company in general insurance broking had joint managing directors, each holding 50%. A dispute broke out, based on one of the parties having an alleged conflict of interest through an intended investment in a related business, which the other party claimed should be part of the existing business. In reality, the non-complainant party was dissatisfied with the complainant's input into the business and wanted to develop his future interests elsewhere.

Following acrimony (with advisers on both sides) it was agreed:
(a) the complainant had an option to buy out the other 50% within 60 days of date of valuation;
(b) the valuation would be independent and binding on both parties, each party having the right to make representations to the valuer;
(c) if the option was not exercised, the other party had an option to buy out the complainant within 30 days, plus a mandatory premium of 15% on the price; and
(d) if neither of the options were exercised, the entire business would be put up for sale.

Representations made to the independent valuer, on behalf of the complainant, included: (1) the usual discount for 50:50 shareholdings should apply; (2) future maintainable profits would drop as the skills and contacts of the outgoing joint managing director were lost to the business.

Representations on behalf of the non-complainant, included: (3) it was a quasi-partnership and no discount should apply; (4) future maintainable net-of-tax profits would increase as the outgoing joint managing partner could be replaced at a lower cost; and (5) the price should reflect a special purchaser as the nature of the business (an easily administered portfolio of recurring insurance commissions) meant there were probably several special purchasers able to 'add-on' this income to their existing business.

The valuer accepted elements of (3) and (4), and rejected (1), (2) and (5). The option was exercised by the complainant. Nearly three years later, the business was sold on a 'rule of thumb' basis of 1.65 times recurring annual commissions (to a special purchaser).

Chapter 9

Valuing a Small Business

Many small businesses cannot be sold in reality.

9-01   It is straightforward to value limited companies of reasonable size, where there is sufficient scale, a range of management and reliable accounting. Valuation is a process of identifying the relevant information and applying marketplace realities to that information.

9-02   A small, sometimes unincorporated, business cannot be valued in the same way as a medium or large business. Valuing such businesses is an occasional, even regular, request for many accounting practitioners. Family disputes, particularly marital separation, and retirement are usually the reason for the valuation of a small business.

9-03   A walk down a street in any town, city suburb or city centre will confirm the prevalence and range of small businesses. Garages, hairdressers, restaurants/takeaways of all kinds, newsagents, repair shops, small pubs and convenience stores are all there.

9-04   These businesses are likely to have a hardworking proprietor. The profits are maybe little more than a quasi-salary for the proprietor. There can be quirks involved, such as separate family ownership of the premises (where there is a limited company), family members on the payroll, non-commercial arrangements with other family interests, and similar. One way or the other, it can be hard to get a fix on a probable recurring level of true profits.

If such a fix on profits can be made (which includes the quasi-salary of the proprietor, who has to be replaced following a sale), it is impossible to find a dependable comparison as to a multiple for valuation purposes, or indeed any form of reliable comparison. The valuation of a small proprietor-led business is light years from a stockmarket multiple or the type of transaction reported in the newspapers.

9–05

Any experienced accounting practitioner will recount that proprietor-led businesses are often not saleable and eventually just disappear on a gradually crumbling basis until finally the pace of change or competition overtakes it, the proprietor falls ill or has had enough. The lack of saleability, and having to explain this to the proprietor, can be difficult for the practitioner in circumstances where the proprietor might have expectations that the sale of the business will fund his retirement.

9–06

Most small businesses have total or almost total dependence on the skills of the proprietor (which would have to be replaced on sale), such as the technical skills for a small engineering business, the chef/proprietor of a restaurant, the buying expertise of the boutique proprietor, and so on. This factor alone mitigates against the business having a saleable value, the business only having a value to the proprietor in its continuity.

9–07

No Active Market

There is no active market for the sale of small businesses and any belief that there is a constant search by active purchasers for such businesses is not true. Neither are larger companies interested in scooping up smaller businesses. It is too much trouble for the return involved, and the 'culture' of the small business is rarely compatible with the larger business.

9–08

Retail businesses of all kinds, such as newsagents, small garages, takeaways and restaurants, are particularly difficult to sell, mainly because banks consider them poor security and will not likely fund a purchase unless there is an underlying freehold property involved.

9–09

Small businesses do not have the capacity to carry bad times, their customer base is limited, banks are restrictive on loans and small scale in itself allows easy entry into the same business by competitors.

9–10　There are no established channels in Ireland for the sale of small businesses, the possibility of a sale being dependent upon the contacts of the proprietor, his accountant and maybe some friends *'who might know somebody who may be interested'*. (There may also be some limited opportunity through a local estate agent or newspaper.) One way or the other, this does not solve the dilemma of the valuation of small businesses.

9–11　The best that might happen is a form of transitory process whereby a purchaser in effect *'buys a job'*, and takes over the business after a period of parallel working alongside the proprietor. Where it does happen it usually involves an employee or relative. The sale terms may centre on the incoming proprietor buying the equipment and stock, and paying the outgoing proprietor a *'consultancy'* for one or two years. One way or the other, whether 'consultancy' or lump sum, the amount involved would likely not exceed the equivalent of one year's pre-tax profits as previously earned by the outgoing proprietor.

9–12　A small business that is capable of an existence independent of the proprietor (meaning that it may be possible to replace his input with a paid manager or that it can be readily merged/added-on to another business) can likely be valued.

9–13　Experience in the marketplace suggests that a small business, with a capability of independent existence, may be valued at up to two times annual sustainable net-of-tax profits. However, this is not always a guideline; such sales are difficult to achieve and usually only happen when a specialist business is involved.

9–14　A complicating factor could be the attitude of third parties to a possible sale. For example, a landlord may not agree to the transfer of a lease, a supplier may restrict credit to a new proprietor, or difficulties may occur on the transfer of some regulatory approval for the business.

Chapter 10

Discounted Cash Flows (DCF)

The use of DCF, as a technique of valuation, is fine in theory, but it has many drawbacks, not least that having arrived at a NPV it is not particularly apparent as to its validity, and what it actually represents, in terms of valuation.

10-01 From time to time there is an attempt to take away, or at least diminish, the judgement aspect of valuation and replace it with some form of arithmetical process or formula. *'Discounted Cash Flows'*, (known as "DCF"), used as a technique of valuation, allows an impression of sophisticated calculations and thereby implies an accuracy in the resultant valuation that is not available through other methods of valuation. In reality, DCF is not as reliable as it might appear, for reasons explained below, and can only be used with any confidence to value a large, stable business with high quality financial information available. The use of DCF is only relevant to 100% company valuations in that it is based on the premise of 100% control over the future cash flows of the company.

10-02 As mentioned at the outset of this book, it is the right to receive future income that is being valued. DCF, as a technique of valuation, is related directly to this fundamental theory of value. Ownership means the right to benefit from the future dividends, retained profits and the proceeds of any future sale. DCF seeks to calculate a *'Net Present Value'* ("NPV") of these benefits as accruing to the potential owner of the business.

10-03 It is necessary to calculate two separate NPVs. One NPV is calculated on a *'stand alone'* basis, that is, without including any synergy or gain arising from the input of the new owner, over and above the existing expected profits. The second NPV includes any such benefits. The important distinction is that the first NPV is the valuation/price to be negotiated with the outgoing owner and the second NPV is the value to the new owner. A moment's thought will demonstrate that a valuation/price based on the second NPV would pay the outgoing owner for the input/expertise of the new owner, though it may still justify paying a slightly higher price than another potential purchaser not able to gain the same synergy.

10-04 The principal advantage of DCF is that it focuses on cash flows rather than on profits alone. Institutional investors are known to carefully review a company's likely future cash flow as an important component in the assessment of the investment potential of a company. Professional investors know that profits, particularly in large and/or diversified companies, are the outcome of increasingly complex accounting and reporting requirements. Profits, referred to as earnings, may not reflect the underlying risks of the business. For example, an apparently profitable and growing business selling higher and higher volumes on credit and/or funding longer-term capital expenditures on short-term funding may be running out of cash. This can happen in any business sector through the mismatching of cash inflows and outflows. In this context, DCF, as a technique of valuation, may also provide an indirect indicator as to the financial risk of the business, which is otherwise not always apparent.

10-05 The basic information required for a DCF valuation is as follows:

- Forecasts of future depreciation, profits and tax on the profits.

- The amounts and timing of capital expenditures. These expenditures may comprise routine replacements and new expenditures (the latter should be evaluated separately in any event).

- The net effect of movements in working capital. This is the area most commonly underestimated or overlooked. It is usually easier to calculate than first appearances may suggest. Relating the components of working capital (debtors, creditors and stocks) to future sales, can normally be based on experience.

- A discount rate, using Present Value Tables (see **Appendix Six**) to calculate today's value of the expected future cash inflows and outflows year-by-year.

The workings of DCF can be complex and particular care is needed as to the validity of the assumptions used. There is a wide range of publications and textbooks available on the topic of DCF.

A major difficulty experienced with DCF is as to the reliability of the underlying information. The apparent sophistication of the DCF method and the necessary calculations can give rise to a misplaced confidence in the outcome. DCF provides the certainty of mathematics but is reliant on the quality of the input information. This information will largely consist of assumptions as to future trading and events over at least 10 years. 10-06

As explained earlier (see **para 3-06**) and repeated below, there is no certainty in business forecasts. Estimating likely future profits is fraught with difficulties, many companies have erratic profit records or the prospects may be significantly better or worse than the historical performance may suggest. The future risk to profits has to be assessed at three levels: 10-07

- The economic outlook, meaning the foreseeable national outlook, including the outlook for overseas markets where relevant. This may include assessment of currency risk.

- Sectoral risk, meaning companies dependent on trends in particular sectors such as construction, agriculture and tourism.

- The specific risk of the business itself. For example, product obsolescence and/or dependence on key customers and/or suppliers.

A common error or fallacy in estimating future profits is to thoughtlessly extrapolate an historical profits progression into an assessment of future profits. This is no more than meaningless 'number crunching'. The mathematics of previous profit progressions (meaning the annual percentage growth over previous years) is an historical outcome and not a perceived certainty or a reasonable assumption as to future performance. It is also the case that, in such circumstances, the percentage growth is being applied to a higher and higher base figure. 10-08

10-09 The discount rate to be applied in itself is a crucial decision and difficult to understand what it is meant to represent. Even a 1% variation in the discount rate, calculated over a long period can have a huge effect on the NPV outcome. This effect is often demonstrated in the calculation comparisons as regards the projected returns from long-term investment in pension funds.

10-10 The information used in the DCF is assembled and tabulated as cash inflows and outflows, year-by-year, over a period of 10 or more years. Included at the end of the final year, as a necessary part of the DCF calculation, is the estimated sale value of the business at that time. This sale value is likely to be some simple multiple of the then forecast annual profits. This sale value, estimated many years ahead, can only be a vague estimate and seems contrary to being a constituent part of a valuation as of now.

10-11 There are no firm guidelines as to an appropriate discount rate. One theory is that the rate should not be less than the investment return that could be obtained on risk-free government bonds (or *'gilts'* as they are commonly known). Probably the most practical approach is to use the interest rate likely to be applicable if the valuation/price was totally borrowed at available rates at the date of valuation.

(See **Appendix Six** for Tables of Present Value (the discount rate).)

10-12 **It will be apparent from the above that the use of DCF as a technique of valuation is fine in theory but it has many drawbacks, not least that having arrived at a NPV its validity, and what it actually represents in terms of valuation, will be open to question. DCF is a highly regarded method of assessing the viability of specific capital projects, where inputs and outputs can be reliably estimated, but attempts to extend it as a universal tool applicable also to the complexities of company valuation/price have not been widely accepted.**

It is also adjused, with some justification in the view of the author, that the difficulties of explaining the concepts of DCF and NPV to a board of directors or to lending bankers, in itself, is a good reason for not using DCF.

Chapter 11

A Quasi-partnership

The leading benchmark in determining the existence of a quasi-partnership is the UK case Ebrahimi v. Westbourne Galleries Ltd *(1972).*

Case law and valuation practice in Ireland and the UK indicate that a minority shareholding may be valued without minority discount in two particular circumstances, namely: **11-01**

- What is known as *oppression of minority*, that is, where the affairs of the company are run to the disadvantage of the minority or, put conversely, that the company is run to the unfair advantage of the majority.

- Where it can be shown that the company, in effect, is what is termed a 'quasi-partnership', meaning that the shareholders could reasonably be described as being in partnership, rather than just fellow shareholders.

The early history of company law shows the concept of joint ownership as being derived from unincorporated trading partnerships. These origins, and the resultant company structures that reflect these origins, can give rise to a sense of partnership in some private companies where all concerned are in effect working partners in the business. **11-02**

The existence of a quasi-partnership is not recognised as such in statutory law, though it is in case law. Whether or not a quasi-partnership exists in a particular set of circumstances will be a matter for legal opinion. The concept of quasi-partnership is well known to legal and accounting practitioners experienced in valuation and in company law. As a result, there is sometimes a rush by advisers to an aggrieved shareholder to deem his shareholding as being part of a quasi-partnership in order to avoid, or at least minimise, a minority discount. **11-03**

11-04 In the experience of the author, the existence of a quasi-partnership is relatively rare. In terms of valuation, a valuer needs to be careful where there is a shareholder dispute with one side saying there is a quasi-partnership and the other side saying there is not. In no circumstances should the valuer place himself in the position of making that decision through his valuation. It is not the role of a valuer to decide whether or not a particular set of circumstances constitutes a quasi-partnership.

11-05 The existence or otherwise of a quasi-partnership will almost inevitably be a matter for legal opinion and/or only be resolved through litigation. An arbitration is the common route to a determination in this regard. It may be that such a determination is carried out first, and the valuer is then instructed as to the basis of valuation.

11-06 A valuer, faced with an unresolved dispute regarding the existence or otherwise of a quasi-partnership, can provide two valuations of the particular shareholding: one on the basis that there is a quasi-partnership, and one on the basis that there is not, the difference between the two valuations likely being the appropriate minority discount.

11-07 The advantage of providing the two valuations is that the valuer is not making the determination as to the existence or otherwise of a quasi-partnership but is providing a framework or range of values for negotiations and possible resolution between the parties.

11-08 The leading benchmark for determining the existence of a quasi-partnership is the 1972 case *"Ebrahimi v. Westbourne Galleries Ltd"*. Though a UK case, it is regularly quoted in Ireland in legal proceedings concerning disputes which involve minority shareholdings.

11-09 That judgment found that the courts could look further than company law rights and entitlements to the background, understandings and relationships between the shareholders, but only in circumstances where it was just and equitable to do so.

11-10 Claims for the existence of a quasi-partnership are usually made parallel to, or as part of, a claim for oppression of minority. It is not certain (in that no judicial decision can be taken as certain in advance) but, where oppression has been proved (or accepted in settlement negotiations), the remedy is almost always that the alleged oppressed shareholding is purchased at proportionate value to the company as a whole without a minority discount **or a smaller than usual discount is applied.**

11-11 In a 2002 case in the UK, *Larkin v. Phoenix Office Supplies Ltd*, the Court of Appeal ruled that the mere fact that a person holds shares in a corporate quasi-partnership does not mean that he can leave the company at will and force the remaining shareholders to purchase his shares at full asset value.

11-12 The facts in each circumstance of alleged quasi-partnership will be different. Experience suggests key features that will influence a determination on the existence or otherwise of a quasi-partnership include the following:

- The ownership history, particularly as to the commencement of the business and the subsequent working roles in the business of individual shareholders.

- The day-to-day decision-making process, i.e. the amount of consultation, however informal, between the management and/or shareholders on everyday decisions.

- The involvement of individual shareholders in the relationship with the company's bankers, including the signing of cheques and personal guarantees.

11-13 There is an Irish case of interest relating to quasi-partnership: *Colgan v. Colgan & Colgan* (1993). A one-third shareholder filed a petition in which he sought relief, pursuant to section 205 of the Companies Act 1963, on the grounds that the respondents (his two brothers owning most of the remaining shares) had conducted the affairs of the company in a manner which was oppressive to the petitioner. The company was engaged in the hotel and licensed trades. The High Court directed the respondents to purchase at a fair value the petitioner's shares in the company. Further, the Court found the fact that a minority interest was being purchased was not a reason for the Court to make a deduction from the valuation of the net assets of the company since the company had been conducted as a quasi-partnership. The complete judgment should be read to understand the full context.

Case History: A Bad Investment

A successful construction/civil engineering company, having undertaken some minor property developments and profitably sold them on, engaged in a 70%:30% joint venture (owning the 70%) with a third party, the intended relationship being that of (70%) construction expertise and (30%) project management/expert knowledge of the nature of the venture. A complicated joint venture agreement governed the relationship between the parties.

The project went disastrously wrong, the costs soared way beyond what was planned and it became evident that the 30% partner had exaggerated its expertise and financial standing. The unfinished project threatened to overwhelm the 70% partner, and bank facilities had been exhausted. The existing shareholders in the (70%) construction company were willing to inject further monies into the project (the 30% shareholder had no money), but such monies were not enough to complete the project, and new outside investors were sought. These investors were sought as investment in the construction company rather than directly for the project.

Complex negotiations took place with potential investors regarding the valuation of the construction company in the circumstances. The outcome was that:

1. the 30% partner discontinued its involvement in the joint venture, its stake was reduced to 15% without any payment and an option on certain terms to purchase this 15% by the construction company was agreed;

2. the construction company, on its own balance sheet, substantially wrote down its financial involvement in the project;

3. the construction company was valued (prior to the injection of new funds) on the basis of five times its likely future maintainable net-of-tax profits (excluding the impact of the project), subject to a cap equal to a 150% premium on the net assets, after the project write-down;

4. a detailed shareholders' agreement was executed between the old and the new shareholders.

Chapter 12

The Special Purchaser

It is generally unwise for a valuer to assume that a potential special purchaser will pay the maximum price, in terms of what the shareholding would be worth to him.

A special purchaser is one who has a particular interest in acquiring a shareholding or the entire company. Such purchasers include the following: **12-01**

- An existing shareholder who, on the acquisition of a further amount of shareholding, would acquire majority control of the company or have a resultant sizeable minority shareholding giving effective control through the other shareholdings being widely dispersed.

- An acquiring company that will be able to make higher profits from the business being purchased, for example by eliminating duplicated costs, gaining economies of scale, selling additional products to customers of the acquired business, etc.

- An acquiring company that will gain a strategic advantage or elimination of an obstruction. Examples include access to a port or distribution facility, acquisition of a licence or a regulatory approval normally subject to a lengthy process, a head start in a particular market, access to advanced technology, etc.

- Where the target company owns property or property rights of particular interest to an acquiring company, such as adjoining land, a right-of-way or the only undeveloped site in a particular location.

In terms of everyday valuation, the possibility of a special purchaser is not likely to exist, though a valuer would nevertheless be wise to consider the existence of such a purchaser, even if not immediately apparent. In any event, it is common valuation practice to include a note in a valuation to the effect that: **12-02**

> "... the valuation does not include the possibility of a special purchaser, should such a purchaser exist, being willing to pay a higher price than shown in this valuation."

12–03 It is generally unwise for a valuer to assume that a potential special purchaser will pay the maximum price, in terms of which the shareholding would be worth to him.

12–04 A potential special purchaser may feel able to pay a higher than normal price for a business, or shareholding in it, for one or more of the reasons mentioned above. Obviously, individual circumstances will vary, but the purchaser taking such an approach to valuation may prove unwise insofar as the potential purchaser could be paying the vendor an enhanced price for the purchaser's own opportunity and expertise, as illustrated by the following example.

> **EXAMPLE**
>
> XYZ Engineering Ltd has future maintainable annual net-of-tax profits of €2.6 million and in the normal way would be valued on a multiple of seven, i.e.
>
> **€2.6 million × 7 = valuation €18.2 million**
>
> ABC Components Ltd expects to enhance the net-of-tax profits of XYZ Engineering Ltd by an additional €1.0 million per year, from €2.6 million to €3.6 million, through savings, improved marketing, etc. On this basis, ABC Components Ltd calculates it could pay (and still not have overpaid for the acquisition):
>
> **€3.6 million × 7 = valuation €25.2 million**
>
> In reality, the above calculation shows that ABC Components Ltd would be paying up to €7.0 million (i.e. the difference between €25.2 million and €18.2 million) to the vendors of

XYZ Engineering Ltd for its own (ABC Components Ltd) opportunities and expertise.

In a competitive market for the acquisition, a higher price than the valuation of €18.2 million could reasonably be paid by ABC Components Ltd. Experience suggests that, in the anxiety to make the acquisition, some purchasers have paid higher than necessary for their own opportunities and expertise.

Chapter 13

A Shareholders' Agreement

The possibility of deadlock is not always addressed in shareholders' agreements.

13-01   The purpose of a shareholders' agreement is to provide protection to minority shareholdings and/or to regulate matters between the differing interests of individual shareholdings. The agreement will also likely give these shareholders a say in the governing and/or management of the company. To that extent, the existence of an agreement will likely have an influence on the valuation of shareholdings in the company. A valuer should always ask if there is a shareholders' agreement in existence.

13-02   A shareholders' agreement is an agreement between (usually) all the shareholders of a private company as to how certain matters (as specified in the agreement) are to be governed in that company. Such an agreement is supplemental to the Articles of Association, though it is important to ensure there is no contradiction between the two documents.

The *'Five Key Provisions'* **in a straightforward shareholders' agreement are summarised on page 95. These cover the basic issues concerning the interests of a minority shareholding, but do not cover the complexity common to agreements where venture capital participation or a joint business venture is involved.**

Legal Advice

13-03   It is necessary to have legal advice in the drafting of an agreement. It is also essential that the agreement is comprehensive, fully completed as to details, and signed by all of the parties. There are regular court cases involving alleged 'agreements' comprising a combination of alleged understandings, drafts that were never progressed, letters or memorandums written at the time, minutes or notes of meetings, etc., which documentation is frequently incomplete, contradictory and/or ambiguous. Often in the good spirit of a new business relationship, some possibly contentious aspects are not carried through to clear documentation.

13-04 A benefit of a shareholders' agreement is that, unlike the Articles of Association, a copy does not have to be filed in the Companies Registration Office and is therefore not a public document. This may not always be clear-cut. If the Articles could not reasonably be interpreted without some of the definitions or explanations in the agreement, it could be said that the agreement is part of the Articles and requires registration. Careful legal drafting should ensure that this will not happen.

13-05 Another obvious reason for seeking legal advice in drafting an agreement is to ensure that its provisions are capable of enforcement. There is little use in having an agreement that is unenforceable in a key provision or, indeed, in its entirety. Company law, competition matters, mergers and acquisitions approvals, even money-laundering, are examples of issues that may have to be addressed in the agreement to ensure its validity.

13-06 The completion of a shareholders' agreement is relatively straightforward. An experienced legal practitioner will readily identify and advise on any unique issues involved, as well as formulate the standard matters normally included in an agreement. (It is money well spent.)

Deadlock

13-07 The possibility of deadlock is not always addressed in shareholders' agreements. Deadlock can happen with 50:50 shareholdings or indeed at any level such as 60:40, 70:30 and so on where the effect is that some proposal or decision is blocked by one or more of the shareholders.

Sometimes such deadlock is contrived to try and force the purchase of the blocking shareholding(s).

13-08 A *'deadlock provision'* can be included in an agreement. A buy/sell option (commonly known as the *'Poker'* or *'Russian Roulette'* option) in the agreement provides that, if there is deadlock (deadlock being defined), one of the parties can serve a notice on the other party stating the price at which he will sell his own shareholding or buy the other party's shareholding (the price per share being the same, whether buying or selling).

13-09 The consequences of serving the notice are that the other party must either sell his shareholding at the stated price or, alternatively, buy the shareholding of the party serving the notice. It can be a clever provision as the price put forward by the person serving the notice would, by and large, have to be a fair price because it is the price at which he might be compelled to sell his own shareholding.

The 'deadlock provision' is not a compulsory mechanism, meaning that the mechanism is there but neither party is obliged to use it in the event of deadlock. However, should one party choose to invoke the mechanism the other party is obliged to either purchase the offered shareholding or to sell his own shareholding.

The willingness to include such a clause in an agreement should depend on the financial strengths of the parties. In the good spirit amongst the parties in setting up the agreement, this aspect may not be given due consideration, a financially weaker party then being at a disadvantage.

13-11 A shareholders' agreement is usually concluded on the commencement of a new business, or on the takeover of an existing business. It is sensible to choose fellow shareholders/investors on the basis of money and expertise, not because of friendship. In the experience of the author, most shareholder fallouts occur between family and/or friends, and not between businesspeople.

The Five Key Provisions in a Shareholders' Agreement

1. x% (commonly 25% or 30%) of net-of-tax profits in a financial year shall be distributed as dividends within nine months after the end of that financial year, provided any previous accumulated losses have been made good, unless shareholdings totalling x% (commonly 80% or 90%) agree otherwise.

This provision underpins value for the minority shareholdings as it provides dividend income.

2. The majority shareholder or shareholders cannot sell their shareholdings to an outside party without obtaining an equivalent pro-rata offer for the minority shareholders.

This provision is known as the *'piggyback'* clause.

3. A restriction on specified major decisions (such as acquisitions or disposals of assets over a certain value, borrowings or guarantees over a certain limit, changes in senior management) unless approved by shareholdings totalling x% (commonly 80% or 90%).

This provision ensures consultation over decisions that may change the risk profile of the company.

4. The appointment of directors. This provision states which shareholders have the right to appoint directors and would include details of remuneration, the financial information to be provided to directors and the number of board meetings to be held each year.

This provision ensures that all shareholders have informed representation on the board.

5. A basis of valuation, and a transfer process, for shareholdings offered for sale to shareholders within the company and to third parties. Almost invariably, approval for the latter will require the unanimous agreement of all the shareholders and would only take place on the basis that the new outside shareholder becomes a party to the shareholders' agreement.

This provision provides a mechanism for the avoidance of some potential disputes regarding valuation.

Chapter 14

Fair Value, Market Value and Willing Buyer / Willing Seller

It is important to recognise that the law on valuation tends to focus on what a purchaser is willing to pay, rather than on what a seller is willing to accept.

14-01   Valuation practitioners differ as to the meaning of *'fair value'*. It is a phrase that regularly crops up in older Articles of Association, in some newer ones as well, in shareholders' agreements, in terms of reference or Letters of Engagement for expert valuers and arbitrators.

14-02   There is no legal definition of 'fair value', though there are a number of indirect references to it in UK court cases, notably the 1954 case *Dean v. Prince*. This case makes particular reference to some of the issues involved in the concept of 'fair value' and should be consulted in complex cases.

> A consensus definition of *'fair value'* amongst practitioners and expert authors in recent times can be stated as follows:
>
> *The definition of fair value is the price at which a shareholding could reasonably be bought or sold in a current transaction between willing parties, that is, other than in a forced liquidation, purchase or sale. The essence of the fair value concept is the desire to be equitable to all of the parties. The fair value concept also assumes that a buyer is unable to obtain the lowest price and that a seller is unable to obtain the highest price.*

There are four points of view that regularly occur amongst practitioners regarding fair value, all being more or less variations on the same theme, which are as follows:

1. That a minority shareholding is just that, a minority shareholding, though fair value indicates that primary regard should be given to an earnings valuation (i.e. not a dividend valuation even if dividends are being paid), with a lesser than normal discount being applied if the acquirer is already a shareholder. This discount would vary as, for example, the acquisition of a 20% shareholding is more important to an existing 35% shareholder than to a 10% shareholder.

2. Similar to 1 above, another view is that the valuation should be fair to both parties, largely interpreted as meaning that any advantage gained by the purchaser (as in the above example) should be shared with the seller.

3. A recognition that there may be, in some cases, an element of quasi-partnership in the relationship between the shareholdings and that a valuation pro-rata to the company as a whole is appropriate. (See **Chapter 11**, Quasi-partnerships.)

4. Where net assets are important, such as in property- or investment-owning companies, a net assets valuation reflecting 1, 2 and 3 above may be relevant. (See **Chapter 6**, The Role of Assets.)

Somewhere between a normal minority valuation (meaning the appropriate discount being applied), and a pro-rata valuation to the whole of the company, is probably the nearest financial calculation of fair value. The valuation would be at its highest where the shareholding being sold will give the purchaser control, or effective control, of the company.

In practice, valuations of fair value often seem to be no more than the amount that the existing shareholders of the company might be willing to pay. This may take the form of a valuer providing an *'indicative value'*, followed by negotiations/mediation between the interested parties.

Legal precedent suggests that a valuer, in providing a fair value valuation, would be wise not to state the reasoning behind his valuation. The *Dean v. Prince* case (see **para 14–02**) is particularly relevant in this context.

14–06 Fair value can be interpreted as being the same as willing buyer/willing seller. Indeed, sometimes terms of reference state that the valuation is to be carried out *'at fair value between willing buyer / willing seller'*.

14–07 The position can be further confused by references to *'market value'* as a basis of valuation. 'Market value', to some valuers, may be the best basis of all for the simple reason that it is purchaser-orientated, the very definition of valuation being what a purchaser is willing to pay. The seller may be willing to sell at this price or he may not. It does not matter; it is the market price.

14–08 The use of *'open market value'* adds to the confusion. Sometimes this is interpreted as meaning the shareholding being sold to anybody who will pay the price, *'market value'* being more confined in terms of the purchaser being an existing shareholder (because of the restriction of the transfer of shares in private companies). There is no statutory definition of either *'market value'* or *'open market value'*, though there are a number of complex UK cases, most of which relate to specific circumstances of general relevance to valuations.

(Much of the case law regarding concepts of value has arisen in the context of tax and can be more readily identified in tax textbooks and journals. Two helpful articles in this regard, "Valuation of Shares" by Denis Cremins, were published in the September 2006 and November 2006 issues of the *Irish Tax Review*.)

14–09 The concept of willing seller/willing buyer is, in essence, a simple proposition, i.e. that a common price will be acceptable to both parties to a transaction. It implies that it is not a forced sale, or that the vendor is not disinclined to sell, and that the purchaser does not have an urgent necessity to buy the shareholding.

14–10 A knock-down figure for the sale of a shareholding with investment uncertainty attached to it would not tempt the owner to sell. Equally, an inflated price that ignores this uncertainty would not find a purchaser. In making a valuation under the aegis of willing seller/willing buyer, it has to be assumed that there are two well-informed and reasonable people of commerce: one willing, but not anxious to sell; and one willing, but not anxious to buy.

It is ultimately the judgement of the valuer as to the interpretation of fair value, market value or willing buyer / willing seller, in particular circumstances.

> **CASE HISTORY: EXCESSIVE BORROWINGS**
>
> A substantial group of companies had a mix of business interests in Ireland and the UK relating to the construction industry. The businesses included manufacturing, distribution and property development. Profitability was erratic.
>
> The manufacturing and distribution businesses were capital intensive, particularly working capital. The activities were largely individually financed with several different banks involved, including extensive use of debtor factoring arrangements. The relatively large scale of the group gave a false sense of security and the fragmented nature of the borrowings and the number of banks involved obscured the fact that total group borrowings were excessive and indeed jeopardised the survival of the group.
>
> A threatened withdrawal of significant facilities by one of the banks precipitated a financial crisis. A new investor, or investors, was urgently sought by the directors. A consortium of investors was found on the basis that the existing group was valued at a multiple of four times the pre-interest and pre-tax profits, and the total borrowings deducted from this figure. This amount, the valuation, was £8.2 million and the new investors put in £3.8 million to give them a pro-rata 32% shareholding (with a detailed shareholders' agreement in place).
>
> Without the excessive borrowings and better management, the valuation of the underlying business would have been considerably higher: probably in excess of £20.0 million.

Chapter 15

A Management Buyout

Experience in the marketplace suggests that the MBO purchase/sale price tends to be in or around the market price.

A *'management buy-out'* ("MBO") is the purchase of a business by some or all of its existing management. As such it is no different than any other purchase/sale of a business.	15–01
In most circumstances, there is no difference in making a valuation for MBO purposes compared to any normal valuation purpose. If anything, there is often more realism to a valuation for an MBO purpose insofar as there is the prospect of an actual purchase/sale.	15–02
The possibility of an MBO can occur for a number of reasons, including:	15–03

- A large organisation, local or multinational, may wish to dispose of an activity/business because it is peripheral to the mainstream business, is an unwanted part of a recent acquisition, the parent needs to raise cash, the activity/business has poor profitability, and so on.
- The owners, often a family, no longer actively run the business and there is pressure from some of the shareholders to realise the capital value of the business.
- The parent is in receivership/liquidation or examinership, and there is potential profitability in one or more of the underlying activities/businesses.

In assessing the valuation of a possible MBO, the earlier commentaries in this book regarding future maintainable profits are highly relevant, particularly the possible adjustments to profitability post the MBO (see **para 3–15**). Venture capitalists often remark that management, in seeking ownership, state that they would run the business quite differently after the acquisition.	15–04

15-05 There are some important factors to consider with regard to any potential MBO:

- The sales relationship with the customers, or a major customer, may be with the outgoing owners.

- Existing suppliers may have been happy to extend extensive credit, in size and payment terms, to the target business when it was part of a large organisation, but may curtail credit under new, less strong ownership.

- Continuance of insurance cover may be at risk for much the same reason as continuing credit from suppliers.

- Similar to the above, financial facilities such as leasing, invoice discounting, seasonal overdraft, may be curtailed on renewal.

15-06 The financing of the MBO may be a mix of promoters' capital (the purchasing management), venture capital, other outside investors, and bank borrowings. Within those forms of capital there are infinite forms of ordinary shares, preference shares, deferred shares, convertible shares, loan stock, mezzanine finance, etc. Mezzanine finance is usually defined as something in between equity and normal bank borrowings. For example, it may be unsecured loan stock with a higher than normal interest rate and with an equity conversion option or a redemption premium.

15-07 Where venture capitalists are involved, there are usually complicated formulae with reference to which the rights, entitlements and options of the different classes of shareholdings are calculated. Reference is sometimes made to positive and negative ratchets whereby the management and/or venture capitalists gain or lose percentage shareholdings according to specific targets as to profits, asset value or debt repayment.

15-08 An argument may be advanced on behalf of management that the sale/purchase price should be less than normal because the vendors may not be providing the usual full warranties and indemnities common to purchase/sale transactions. This will be a matter for negotiation. In practice, there appears to be no significant reduction, the reason being that likely pitfalls should be known to management and already factored into the purchase/sale price.

15–09 Similarly, there is the uneasy relationship that develops between owners and management when an MBO is mooted. Sometimes the vague or express threat of a management walkout to establish a rival business may be used when negotiating the sale/purchase price. It is not the role of the valuer, in some way or other, to evaluate such a threat when considering his valuation.

15–10 The owners of a business always have the option to sell to whosoever they please and owners will almost invariably seek advice/look to the marketplace before selling to management. Experience in the marketplace suggests that the MBO sale/purchase price tends to be in or around the market price.

15–11 The main issue in an MBO is agreement on the percentage shareholdings between the purchasing parties. The management will likely have limited cash resources compared to outside investors but will naturally seek a disproportionately higher percentage of the total equity. The common solution is to have management allocated the equivalent of, say, €1.25 in shareholding for each €1.00 invested, with options to increase shareholdings on advantageous terms subject to the achievement of specific targets.

15–12 Even if there are no outside shareholders involved in the MBO, the completion of a comprehensive shareholders' agreement is essential. The interests and priorities of an employed manager are different to those of an owner/manager. The strains and stresses of managing a business where there may be personal liabilities due to borrowings, plus individual perceptions/beliefs as to the strategic management of the business, can lead to disputes.

15–13 The resignation, ill-health or death of a shareholder/manager and the consequent sale or transfer of their shareholdings to family members will, in time, dissipate the commonality of the founding shareholders/managers. It is also the case that subordinate shareholders/managers to the chief executive can perceive themselves as his employer, with the consequent

15-14 THE VALUATION OF BUSINESSES AND SHARES

difficulty in seeking consensual decisions in the running of the business.

15-14 In summary, the valuation of a business for a possible MBO is no different than the normal valuation carried out for the purpose of indicating an appropriate sale price.

Chapter 16

Intellectual Property

It is reported in the United States that once a technology-based company reaches annual sales of US$10 million, the founders want to sell, and/or raise new equity, up to 25% of its value.

16-01 The term 'intellectual property' cannot be precisely defined but is generally accepted to include the following:

- Patents
- Copyright
- Trademarks
- Registered designs
- Technical know-how
- Research & Development

Brands (such as newspaper titles or well-known product names) are also referred to as intellectual property, though such are perhaps more properly described as intangible assets.

16-02 The growth in intellectual property from the early 1990s onwards has been remarkable, increasing every day in innovativeness, range and complexity. Sometimes the intellectual property is extremely valuable, a feature that may only become apparent in the process of creating that property and/or when the product becomes known in the marketplace.

16-03 Intellectual property carries legal complexity with it. A valuer, in circumstances where the ownership and/or the use of intellectual property is integral to the operations and/or well-being of a company, would be well advised to seek expert legal and technical advice thereon.

16-04 It is frequently the case, in technology-based companies, that company valuations are sought for the purpose of raising further equity funding to continue/advance the necessary research and development through to completion.

16-05 The dilemma for the valuer can be that he is presented with accounts showing little trading, accumulated losses, and forecasting heavy expenditures on uncompleted research and development, together with a set of what may be stratospheric sales projections for the claimed end product. The technology bubble of the late 1990s/early 2000s has, however, made potential investors much more wary as to such forecasts and projections.

16-06 Not all circumstances are like the foregoing. A company may hold valuable intellectual property rights, which have not been fully exploited, for whatever reason, and which have good long-term potential.

16-07 From the valuer's point of view, it is the likely income and/or protection involved that is of particular interest. For example, a company successfully selling a patented widget has *'pricing power'* (see **paras 3–16** and **3–17**) and market monopoly. The company is therefore likely to have a higher value than if it did not have the patent protection for its future income.

16-08 The valuation of an income stream arising from the licensing out of the intellectual property will greatly depend on the details of the legal and technical agreements such as tenure, minimum/maximum payments involved and restrictions. The financial strength and the market capabilities of the licensee would be an important factor in a valuation.

16-09 Commentaries and studies following the boom and bust era of technology stocks in the late 1990s/early 2000s suggest that the survivors were those companies that had identified in advance the probable specific users/markets for their completed products, knew what the competition was, and legally protected their products. The technology companies thereby found that the established market rules on business survival and success applied to them as well.

16-10 The valuer of an embryonic or even an established technology company would be wise to assess the particular company in the context of the foregoing experiences. Technology companies, unlike the more established business sectors, can do spectacularly well, and quickly. However, experience has shown that major profitability, often confined to just one product and its derivations, can evaporate in a short period unless there is constant innovation and new products coming on stream.

16–11 There are insufficient published transactions regarding the sale of technology-based companies to form any guidelines on valuations. Some venture capital companies have developed a good working knowledge as to the likely success or otherwise of technology-based companies in particular sectors. However, this expertise is not common knowledge.

Chapter 17

A Professional Practice

There is no identifiable 'norm' as to the valuation of a professional practice. A valuation is usually achieved through negotiation / mediation between the interested parties.

17-01 Professional practices cannot be valued on the same basis as trading companies. A professional practice gives the appearance of a life independent of ownership/management, such as for a company, but in fact a professional practice has no legal personality and is no more than self-employed individuals (sole traders) earning a living, either individually (in a sole practice) or collectively (in a partnership).

The valuation of a professional practice is rarely straightforward. Each practice has its own individual circumstances and characteristics. An understanding that partnership law is quite different to private company law is essential to the valuation of a professional practice.

17-02 Professionals normally trade as individuals or in partnerships. Trading through limited companies is common for property/construction-related professionals such as consulting engineers, architects, quantity surveyors and estate agents. Solicitors and accountants do not trade as limited companies, though sometimes the latter may carry out some of their business through a limited company for management consultancy, company secretarial services, and other non-auditing/accounting activities.

17-03 Sole practices are usual in the medical and veterinary professions, though general practice partnerships in those professions are becoming increasingly common. Barristers trade as individuals.

There is no value to the practice of a barrister or a medical consultant, except in its continuity to the individual, as the clients and expertise are not transferable. There is no apparent formula or *'norm'* for the valuation/sale of medical and dental general practices. In some cases, a sale is restricted by the inability to transfer lists of public patients'. Any value in a general medical or dental practice, with a good level of recurring private patients, is usually related to the *'head start'* it provides to a purchaser. This value appears to be circa one year's private patient fees, simply on the basis that experience suggests that this seems to be acceptable to sellers and purchasers, with separate purchase of equipment and the value of a lease (if any).

17-04

Practice, in all professions, is competitive and a partnership needs to constantly assess the right balance between *'finders, grinders and minders'*, that is, those who get new clients, those who do the work and those who manage the firm. A sole practitioner has to be all of those things. The pace of change, particularly in the regulatory environment, changes in legislation and in the development of skills, means constant learning and adaptation. Change is much more pronounced in professional practice than in the general run of business life.

17-05

A partnership is a relationship founded on mutual trust and good faith. In law, every partner is liable jointly and severally with the other partners for all debts and obligations incurred while he is a partner. Partners are jointly and severally liable for frauds, breaches of trust, torts or misrepresentations committed by other partners in the course of business.

17-06

The Partnership Act 1890

Partnership law has remained virtually unchanged since it was encoded in the Partnership Act 1890. Short and written clearly, the Act covers three main areas: relations between partners; relations with clients and other third parties; and dissolution. The Act makes no mention of goodwill or the valuation of a practice. It is, however, necessary to have a good working knowledge of

17-07

17-08 THE VALUATION OF BUSINESSES AND SHARES

the Act in order to advise on the issues that arise in a partnership dispute/valuation of a practice.

(See **Appendix Five** for the Partnership Act 1890.)

17-08 The Act contains few provisions that cannot be altered by agreement between the partners. In effect, the Partnership Act 1890 regulates partnerships unless overridden by agreement of the partners. Note that a course of action carried out over time may constitute an agreement between partners, though not always. It is best to have a written partnership agreement, preferably a comprehensive partnership agreement, drawn up with legal guidance, in order to cover the eventualities that will occur in every partnership over time.

(A useful Irish book on partnership is Michael Twomey, *Partnership Law* (Butterworths, 2000).)

17-09 The subsequent Limited Partnership Act 1907 fulfils a different purpose and is rarely relevant to professional partnerships.

Partners Come and Go

17-10 In the normal life of a partnership, new partners join and existing partners leave, fall ill, retire or die. Rarely is a partner expelled as this is fraught with legal difficulties. Practices expand, shrink, change direction, merge, de-merge, are sold or disappear altogether. A sole practitioner has control of events, but he too needs guidance regarding valuation when taking on a partner, merging or selling the practice.

17-11 Few partnership agreements state that a partner can be expelled for poor performance (as opposed to fraud or malpractice) because of the difficulties in defining poor performance and also because of a general unwillingness to sign an agreement with such a clause in it. The result is usually acrimony, followed by hostile negotiations to persuade a partner to leave in such circumstances.

17-12 A partner cannot be expelled for poor performance or forced to retire unless the power to do so has been conferred by express agreement between the partners. In carrying out the latter, under common law, equity and natural justice the partners must act in complete good faith. Using legal threats to force out a partner, where there is no express agreement, is of no value, as a court has power only to dissolve the partnership, not expel a partner.

17-13 If the problems cannot be resolved by agreement, then there will have to be full dissolution. This will necessitate a sale of all the assets of the partnership, including work-in-progress and goodwill, if necessary by a receiver appointed by the court.

17-14 Retirement of a partner is perhaps the most common problem and there is a contemporary trend towards earlier retirement, even in the professions. Many practitioners do not provide adequately for their retirement. The incentive to retire is not there in such circumstances, causing friction with the other partners. In the absence of an explicit partnership agreement covering the issue, the remaining partners may be faced with demands from the outgoing partner for a capital sum and/or a pension. These demands, realistic or otherwise, are in effect a claim as to valuation by the outgoing partner of his interest in the practice.

17-15 What may comes as a surprise to some professional practitioners is that the Act provides that a partnership can be immediately terminated (dissolution) by notice given by any one partner to all the others – written notice is not needed, nor is there a required period of notice. A partner can attend a partners' meeting and announce that the partnership is now at an end. This is in the absence of a written agreement to the contrary.

17-16 There is nothing that can be done about this dissolution, a court is powerless to intervene in the absence of alleged misdemeanour or fraud. The bank account is frozen, the employees are made redundant and the relationship with clients is automatically terminated. If the (now) former partners cannot agree on how to deal with the dissolution, as mentioned earlier, a receiver will be appointed by the court to dispose of the assets and discharge the liabilities.

17-17 In reality, few such dissolutions take place as it is rarely in anybody's interest to do so. In the absence of a written partnership agreement covering the point, the threat of dissolution can be used by an unreasonable partner to force a particular course of action, usually to his advantage.

A Partnership Agreement

17-18 The completion of a partnership agreement is, therefore, a sensible course of action, not only as regards possible dissolution but also to avoid the pitfalls and problems identified in this chapter. Appropriate legal and tax advice should be sought in drafting a partnership agreement.

It is not unusual to find a partnership agreement with ill-thought-out clauses stating an unrealistic and costly basis of valuing goodwill when calculating payment to an outgoing partner. This is particularly so where there are founding partners more advanced in age than subsequent younger partners and the agreement was drawn up to the advantage of the former.

17-19 All partnerships, irrespective of profession, carry potential problems. Indeed, without a clear and comprehensive partnership agreement, a partnership is likely to carry the seeds of its own destruction. Otherwise prudent and competent professional practitioners have been caused serious distress, sometimes late in their careers, through not taking the time to properly organise their partnership affairs.

17-20 A partnership agreement could not cover all possible eventualities. As mentioned earlier (**para 17-12**) it is usually impossible to agree on a clause enabling expulsion of a partner for poor performance. This is because of difficulties in defining poor performance and, indeed, a reluctance to sign an agreement with such a clause. In this context, it should be noted that the Partnership Act 1890 is not the complete law on partnership. The rules of equity and common law continue to apply as follows:

> *"The rules of equity and common law applicable to partnership shall continue in force except as far as they are inconsistent with the express provisions of this Act".*
> (Section 46 of the Partnership Act 1890)

Goodwill

17-21 All of the foregoing raises the vexed question as to whether or not a professional practice has a value and, if so, how it is best measured. In this context, the term '*goodwill*' has traditionally been associated with professional practice. Goodwill was discussed earlier (**paras 6–21** to **6–30**) and it is useful to repeat here the definition of goodwill *per* Lord Eldon in *Cruttwell v. Lye* (1810):

> "... *nothing more than the probability that the old customers will resort to the old place even though the old trader or shopkeeper has gone*".

This was reinforced by Lord McNaghten's definition in *IRC v. Muller* (1901):

> "... *the benefit of good name, reputation and connection of a business. It is the attractive force which brings in custom*".

17–22 The goodwill of a practice exists to the extent there is a continuing business. A practice is built up over time, and risk undertaken, and an outgoing partner may hold the view that his efforts in building-up the business should be recognised through a value placed on his share of the profits, profits which may accrue in the future to the continuing partners. The same could be said for an incoming partner asked to pay for goodwill. Translated into monetary terms, 'goodwill' is only the measure of future extra profits, not the total profits previously earned by the outgoing partner.

17–23 Consider the example of a retiring partner earning profits of €xxxx a year. On first glance, it may appear the remaining partners will gain €xxxx a year between them and that, therefore, a valuation based on a multiple of those profits (a capital value) should be paid to the outgoing partner, similar to the valuation of a business in a private company.

17–24 A valuation, of a professional practice is not that straightforward. The previous work input of the outgoing partner in earning continuing profits has to be replaced by an increased workload on others. Professional responsibilities are high and the work may not be easily handled by or delegated to the remaining partners. The profits previously earned will not accrue passively in the future. It is reasonable to expect that profits will drop in the future as the particular skills and contacts of the outgoing partner are lost. This aspect is intangible, but experience suggests such loss may take 12 to 18 months to become apparent. There is

17-25 THE VALUATION OF BUSINESSES AND SHARES

a certain momentum attached to existing professional work but which only carries so far into the future unless it is replenished.

> **CASE HISTORY: THE DEATH OF A PARTNER**
>
> A four-partner professional practice, established 16 years previously by John, was prosperous and expanding. John died suddenly at age 49. The remaining partners, Peter, David and Paul, paid John's capital account to his estate but refused to make any payment for goodwill and continued the practice. There was no partnership agreement. Profit shares had been John 40%, Peter 20%, David 20% and Paul 20%. Threatened legal action by the executor of John's estate resulted in the *'fair value'* of goodwill being referred to arbitration.
>
> Following detailed submissions, oral and written, the arbitrator held: (1) there was a value to the goodwill acquired by the continuing partners following the death of John; (2) allowing for the loss of John's skill and contacts, together with the cost of the necessary replacement work input, the continuing partners nevertheless stood to gain additional annual profits equivalent to 20% of total partnership pre-tax profits; (3) this 20% annual profits share was to be calculated on the average annual profits for the last three accounting years prior to John's death; (4) the appropriate value, or multiple, was 1.75 times this profit share.

17-25   Goodwill in a professional practice is only the measure of extra profits. This is defined to the effect that there is no goodwill in an income is not greater than that which could be earned by employment elsewhere without the risk of professional responsibilities. The purchase of goodwill, without such extra profits, would be the equivalent of buying a job.

Restricted Market

17-26   The purchase/sale of a business is normally carried out on an open market basis between a willing buyer/willing seller. Practitioners familiar with the valuation of private company shares will know that a lesser value must apply where there are restrictions on open sale. In placing a valuation on an interest in a partnership, it can be said that there is a willing buyer (the remaining partners) and a willing seller (the outgoing partner). That circumstance in itself does not represent what is generally understood by open market. Instead, it may be seen as captive seller and/or captive buyer. Open market, as commonly interpreted, is also restricted through a purchaser having to possess the appropriate professional qualification.

17-27 It is fundamental to a valuation of any business that what is being valued is the right to receive future income. A professional practice is no different in this respect. The continuing partners could not reasonably be expected to pay for the outgoing partner's share of the practice unless there was the expectation of it generating future profits for them (the definition of future profits is discussed below at **paras 17-32** to **17-34**. The same could be said for a new partner asked to pay for goodwill.

17-28 A professional practice cannot be valued on the same basis as shares in a company. The circumstances are completely different. Sometimes one hears that the valuation of a professional practice is a multiple of annual fees. This can be true (see **para 17-04**). However, there are insufficient publicly-known transactions in what is not an open market for a consensus on valuation to have emerged. There are no definitive formulas available except the expertise/experiences of valuation practitioners. Nevertheless, there are some identifiable features and parameters common to most valuations as explained in this chapter. The case histories herein demonstrate some familiar situations.

The Return is Uncertain

17-29 Common sense suggests that it is unwise to value the relevant future pre-tax profits on a multiple greater than 2. In many instances, the multiple would be less. Allowing personal tax on the future income at, say 40%, it would therefore take 3.3 years after-tax profits for the purchaser(s) to recover the capital costs based on a multiple of 2. This is the time that would elapse before the purchaser would receive a return over and above the capital cost paid.

17-30 The return over and above the capital paid is uncertain. The *'asset'* being acquired is intangible, with no physical assets such as a building, debtors, to back it up. Sustained work input by the purchaser(s) (the remaining partners) will be necessary to earn the future profits. Even then, there are no guarantees or certainties; circumstances can quickly change and clients can leave at any time.

17-31 There is consensus among valuation practitioners that 'goodwill' does not have a monetary value to an individual partner in a large professional practice. This is because the ability/expertise to handle large and/or highly complex transactions, and the established reputation of the practice is such that goodwill does not exist to an extent attributable to an individual partner. The need to attract and hold new talent in such practices also mitigates against payment for goodwill by incoming partners. Partnership agreements in large legal and accountancy practices normally specify that goodwill has no monetary value and is only vested in the continuing partners.

17-32 Ascertaining future maintainable profits, an essential step in any valuation, invariably causes difficulty, if not outright disagreement, in the valuation of an interest in a professional practice. As stated repeatedly in this book, what is being valued is the right to receive that income.

> **CASE HISTORY: THE RETIREMENT OF A PARTNER**
>
> In a long-established professional practice with two senior partners, aged 68 and 64, and four junior partners aged between 34 and 46, there was a partnership agreement which did not cover retirement or goodwill except to state that the two (founding) senior partners *"retained the value of the practice"* for themselves. The two senior partners owned the practice offices, rented to the partnership in the normal way.
>
> The senior partner, aged 68, suddenly announced he wished to retire and sell his *"50% share of the practice"* to the four junior partners, one of which was his son. The price mentioned was 50% of 1.5 times the average annual gross fees of the practice over the previous three years. The senior partner said that his son was not expected to pay his share – it was being

gifted. No basis was advanced for this valuation. At the time, each of the two senior partners had a 23% share of profits; the remaining four partners shared as to 15%:13%:13%:13%.

Acrimony ensued and the situation was only resolved when three junior partners, excluding the son, verged on setting up a new practice. The settlement was that the practice continue as previously, with each senior partner to retire at 70 as part of a complicated arrangement whereby no capital sum was paid on retirement but each received a profit share of 11% for life or 10 years, whichever was the shorter. The profit shares of the senior partners, on retirement or death, were to be divided equally amongst the four junior partners, which included the son.

17-33 A first draft of what might be future maintainable profits will demonstrate the equivalent of maybe 50% to 60% of the previous year's fee income in a solicitors' practice as likely to recur in the coming 12 months, probably higher for an accountants' practice. An established solicitors, or accountants, practice, unless declining through special circumstances or the advanced age of a practitioner, tends to be reasonably stable in year-to-year fee income despite the apparent *'once-off'* nature of much of the work. Analysis of the fee income for the past two-to-three years will identify any large 'once-off' fees or the gain/loss of a major recurring client.

17-34 In estimating future maintainable profits it should be borne in mind that a practice requires finance. A partner leaving the practice will be repaid his capital account. This will mean a replacement financing burden on the continuing partners that can only be met by new capital from the continuing partners, bank borrowings and/or reduced drawings by the continuing partners.

EXAMPLE: CALCULATION OF FUTURE ANNUAL MAINTAINABLE PROFITS

In a five-person professional partnership, a 20% partner is ceasing practice. Financial year-end is 30 April and the cessation date is 31 December 20xx.

> 20% profit share: year ended 30 April 20xx: €80,046
> 20% profit share: year ended 30 April 20xx: €67,670
> 20% profit share: year ended 30 April 20xx: €84,312
>
> (the last year is an estimate of the outcome for the current financial year ending 30 April 20xx)
>
> In the second year ended 30 April 20xx above, there was an exceptional cost of fitting out new offices written off as an expense in that year; 20% of the cost write-off in that year was €17,488. A simple annual average (after making this adjustment) over the three years is pre-tax profits of €83,172, attributable to the outgoing partner.
>
> 85% of this annual average €83,172 is thought to be maintainable, i.e. €70,696. Related input costs are estimated at €42,242, resulting in estimated future maintainable pre-tax profits of €28,454 accruing to the continuing partners. A multiple of one to two would therefore give a *'goodwill'* valuation in the range €28,454 to €56,908.

Mergers

17-35 There are few professional practices of good size that have not, along the way, merged with or acquired another practice. Indeed, there are probably few practitioners who have not contemplated, however tentatively, a merger or acquisition at some time or other. Contemplation of a merger involves some form of evaluation / valuation of the respective practices.

17-36 The reasons or circumstances that create mergers include the following:

- **Scale of activity** The need to offer a range of services and/or the necessity of scale to attract and hold sizeable clients.
- **Skills and knowledge** It is critical to keep pace with the growing complexity of the business world. For professional practices, this necessitates continuing professional education at a high level, and frequent updating of technology. Often, only practices of a certain size can afford the related costs.

- **Professional Regulation** Regulation has greatly increased, both internal and external to the professions. Compliance is time-consuming, requires skilled input, and is costly to smaller practices.
- **Age profile and succession** It is not unusual, even in some large practices, for the partners to be clustered around a particular age. This not only creates succession problems in terms of hindering accession by younger talent, but also sometimes leads to resistance to, or a lack of recognition of, change.

> *It is true to say that most mergers of professional practices are contemplated defensively: on the one hand to share fixed costs and reduce variable costs through economies of scale, thereby hopefully maintaining and improving profitability; and, on the other hand, to alleviate the difficulties of coping with professional regulatory compliance and to keep pace with the complexities of a fast-changing business environment.*

17-37 Mergers of professional practices do not always bring the expected benefits. A merger for ill-defined reasons or with unrealistic expectations (such as an expectation that the merger will solve cash-flow problems) on either side, can be costly. It is not that the practices will subsequently de-merge (the integration will likely be only reversible at considerable cost), but that there may well be an unpleasant upheaval within the merged entity, probably within 12 to 18 months.

17-38 Problems that occur through bad planning, leading to later difficulties, include:

- **Too many partners** This is best addressed sooner rather than later. Overlapping skills and areas of responsibility are the most frequent problems in this respect. Obviously, it can be difficult to obtain the agreement of a partner to a merger in which he will become redundant, but it is a fact of life and must be addressed accordingly.
- **Loss of clients** Client perceptions of the merger, conflicts of interest, changes in personnel handling their accounts, all contribute to the loss of clients.

17-39 THE VALUATION OF BUSINESSES AND SHARES

- **Demotivation of employees** Staff may interpret the merger as a threat to their jobs or positions, particularly in circumstances where the merger is mooted on the basis of increased productivity or cost savings. Good staff may seek jobs elsewhere.

- **Management of the merger** The post-merger situation requires considerable efforts to ensure that the expected benefits are actually achieved. Sometimes there is a sense of relief that the merger was achieved at all, and matters subsequently drift in an aspirational but inconclusive way.

- **Culture shock** The philosophy of different practices can vary widely. For example, individual partners may be unused to time-recording or strict billing procedures, might be systems illiterate, have poor professional standards, be bad record-keepers, or do not keep abreast of necessary knowledge.

17-39 For all of the above reasons and more, practices contemplating a merger should engage a professional intermediary (professional bodies will informally recommend a suitable person) to act on their behalf in sourcing potential merger candidates and to initiate discussions.

17-40 This intermediary should obviously be experienced enough to understand the issues involved, undertake whatever reviews or investigations are necessary, and generally carry the merger (assuming a suitable candidate for a merger is identified and willing to proceed) to a successful conclusion, including planning for the post-merger era in order to achieve the expected benefits.

17-41 It is always of great assistance if each of the practices seeking to merge appoints such an intermediary. Professional practitioners, because they act as advisers to their clients, feel competent to undertake merger discussions themselves. This is understandable, but objectivity may be lost and, having regard to what is at stake, it is wise to stand back from the fray and for each party to engage a competent adviser. Such an adviser, in any event, cannot make any commitments and can only act on instructions, so there is little risk in such an appointment.

> **CASE HISTORY: THE MERGER OF PRACTICES**
>
> Two professional practices sought to merge. Both had done well in the past but each found it increasingly difficult to provide comprehensive client services and to cope with strong competition. The proposed merger was defensive. The result of the proposed merger would be nine partners, with a serious age imbalance. Three were in their 30s, five were aged late 40s/early 50s and one aged 61. It was evident there would be too many partners in the merged practice. Neither practice had a partnership agreement.
>
> An independent adviser (agreed by both parties) to the merger identified four partners as having overlapping skills compared to the likely mix of future business. Two partners in their late 40s agreed to leave with a "*package*" equivalent to 1.5 times their latest gross annual earnings. This was paid by a 40% immediate lump sum and 60% in "*standby*" consulting fees at the rate of 2% per month for 30 months. Each undertook not to approach any client of the practice, except for those on a specific shortlist, for 18 months. As a separate matter, the partner aged 61 agreed to retire at 63 with a two-year part-time consultancy agreement.

A Non-performing Partner

17-42 Circumstances change and individual partners sometimes do not keep pace. The result is pressure from the other partners for the non-performing partner or partners to leave the practice, which can become acrimonious. As a partner cannot be forced to retire, or be expelled, unless there is a partnership agreement covering this specific circumstance, the result is usually an acrimonious negotiation of compensation (usually related to a valuation of the practice, though such may not be the complete picture) to persuade the particular partner or partners to leave the practice.

17-43 In many cases, the outgoing partner wishes to continue earning his living in professional practice. Part of the solution may be that the outgoing partner, by agreement, takes a specified list of clients to his new practice on the assumption that those clients will be willing to transfer, and that the continuing partners will not hinder such transfer.

17-44 It is usual that the outgoing partner's capital account is repaid, plus interest, at intervals over a period of (say) two or three years. Sometimes it might be agreed that, say, 25% of the capital account is payable immediately on the signing of the cessation agreement. This is usually done in circumstances where the outgoing partner may have outstanding personal tax that would normally be paid from the partnership and/or to provide some funding for a new practice.

17-45 Inevitably, there will be arguments between the outgoing partner and the continuing partners as to the value, if any, attributable to goodwill. (The issue of goodwill in professional practice is covered earlier in this Chapter.) Where agreed, the transfer of on-going clients to the outgoing partner tends to be the *'equivalent compensation'* for goodwill, though a relatively small capital sum may be negotiated as well.

17-46 Where there is disagreement and acrimony, it is sensible to appoint an agreed mediator to assist in resolving the conflict. A professional body can informally recommend an experienced mediator. It is also necessary to recognise that, almost inevitably, the particular partner or partners must leave the partnership as the necessary trust between all concerned has broken down. If an outside mediator is not successful, it will probably be necessary to agree on arbitration. Experience suggests that it can take some time to agree terms of reference for an arbitration because one or both parties will seek to have terms that in themselves are a vindication of the validity of the claim(s) being made.

17-47 When a partner leaves a solicitor's practice it is common to include a clause whereby he would eventually receive an agreed share of fees from specified litigation cases as and when such fees are received. This usually arises in circumstances of long-tailed litigation where there is uncertainty as to the outcome.

17-48 The value attributable to work-in-progress, and the outgoing partner's share in it, may also be a matter of contention. A partnership will have adopted a policy over time on the valuation of work-in-progress in its annual accounts. Unless there is a compelling reason otherwise (such as long-tailed litigation mentioned above), it is difficult to accept that such policy should be amended simply because of a change in the partnership. Sometimes the solution is to agree an additional X months' future profits, to be paid to the outgoing partner, as being the value of understated work-in-progress.

There are tax implications arising from any change in policy on valuing work-in-progress. There are various guidelines followed by the tax authorities on the preparation of professional accounts which include the treatment of work-in-progress, and these should be followed. **17–49**

Any capital sum payments to an outgoing partner for goodwill are not tax deductible to the continuing partner or partners but may be taxable in the hands of the recipient. As part of the settlement with an outgoing partner, to include goodwill and work-in-progress, it is often agreed to pay the outgoing partner consultancy fees over a period. However, the tax position in this regard needs to be carefully considered. **17–50**

> **CASE HISTORY: EXPULSION**
>
> A four-partner professional practice, with a large volume of business, had poor profitability due to a predominance of low-fee work. The practice was under financial pressure as a result, aggravated by large borrowings following the fitting-out of expensive new rented premises two years previously.
>
> One partner, John, had a seriously overdrawn capital account arising from an expensive lifestyle. There were large travel and entertainment bills regularly presented by this partner as necessary marketing expenditure for the practice. The other partners alleged that John made an inadequate contribution to the practice, and considerable difficulties, with legal advisers on each side, followed an attempt to expel John without compensation. There was no partnership agreement.
>
> The eventual compromise involved:
>
> 1. John taking specified clients, but approaching no others, to a new practice;

> 2. John continuing as a guarantor on the premises lease for five years;
>
> 3. the overdrawn capital account being repaid in full within 30 days;
>
> 4. the specified clients could not be approached by John until his overdrawn capital account was paid in full.

Valuation of a Sole Practice

17-51 The primary reason for buying a sole practice is to obtain *'a head start'* and shorten the time necessary to establish a practice. In general, though not an active or identifiable market, it appears that there is a greater demand than supply for the purchase of established sole solicitor and accountant practices.

17-52 The valuation of a sole practice can be straightforward; a sale on the open market will dictate the price. A practitioner wishing to sell his practice may first need guidance on the asking price. The same practice may be more attractive to one purchaser than another. For example, a practice that could profitably be added to an existing practice may be more valuable sold that way than being sold to an individual commencing in practice. The sale of a deceased person's practice can present obvious difficulties in continuity compared to that of a retiring practitioner.

17-53 In selling/purchasing a sole practice, a factor not always recognised is a possible generation gap. Clients generally are more comfortable doing business with somebody around their own age. An age profile of clients in a sole practice will often show a preponderance in the age bracket of five years either side of the practitioner's age. A younger person buying an older person's practice may, therefore, not have as much continuity as past fee income might suggest.

17-54 The ability to finance the purchase will restrict the price a potential purchaser is willing to pay. Aspiring accountants and solicitors are viewed favourably by banks because of the possibility of further business accruing to the banks. Lending to other professions for practice purchase tends to be more cautious.

17-55 For a new entrant to practice, it seems that banks will expect the potential purchaser to provide at least one-third of the price from his own resources, with the balance of two-thirds being capable of repayment on a term-loan basis over, say, five to seven years. Annual capital repayments would be expected not to exceed 15% to 20% of pre-tax earnings, (i.e. profits after all expenses including interest).

17-56 Routine office equipment and fittings used in the practice may be included in the purchase price, but not expensive computers and software. Work-in-progress would not be included. This is valued separately at the take over date and paid over to the outgoing practitioner as realised. Debtors belong to the outgoing practitioner, who is liable to discharge the outstanding creditors of the practice.

17-57 Sole practices are usually sold on the basis of deferred purchase price payments. This may be accomplished in tandem with a transition period with the incoming and outgoing practitioners working alongside. A transition period will normally prove necessary in any event, not only to familiarise the incoming practitioner, but also to minimise loss of clients.

17-58 The value of a sole accountancy practice tends to be based on a multiple of gross annual recurring fees, rather than on the *'earnings valuation'*. There is no absolute rule, but experience suggests that sellers and purchasers find it comfortable to adopt the following formula, or something similar:

Gross annual recurring fees (individual clients)	Valuation
Up to €10,000	€0.75 in the €1.00
€10,000 to €25,000	€1.00 in the €1.00
Over €25,000	€1.25 in the €1.00

Example: a client with gross annual recurring fees of €30,000 would be valued at €30,000 × 1.25 = €37,500

> **EXAMPLE: CALCULATION OF MAXIMUM BORROWINGS FOR THE PURCHASE OF A SOLE ACCOUNTANT'S PRACTICE**
>
> Expected future pre-tax earnings following
> purchase of practice   €75,000 pa
>
> Bank capital repayments: (say) maximum
> 20% of pre-tax earnings of €75,000 pa   = €15,000 pa
>
> €15,000 pa bank capital repayments for say
> six years: total   = €90,000
>
> The maximum bank borrowings would therefore be €90,000, being two thirds of the purchase price. The total maximum purchase price would thus be:
>
> $$\frac{€90,000 \times 3}{2} = €135,000$$
>
> The €135,000 purchase price would represent a purchase price of 1.8 times pre-tax profits.
>
> *The above is a general illustration and not definitive. Broadly, it appears that a sole practice has a value of not more than twice maintainable pre-tax profits. A formula based on recurring fees (see **para 17-58**) seems to generally give about the same valuation.*

17-59 The sale/purchase of a sole solicitor's practice cannot be as readily valued as an accountant's practice. Experience suggests that purchasers and sellers are comfortable with a multiple of gross recurring fees (GRF). This is normally calculated by taking an annual average of the gross fees over the previous three years prior to sale, adjusted for unusual or non-recurring circumstances.

17-60 The multiple might be up to 1.00 times the GRF fees for a well-established (20 years or more) practice, with a practice of less than 10 years probably having substantially less value. The valuation also greatly depends on the mix of the practice, some practices obviously having a greater chance of recurring business than others. A multiple of 0.75 to 1.00 times GRF appears to be a common valuation range for established practices in terms of the market willingness to buy and sell in that range.

Work-in-progress would be valued at the date of sale/purchase and normally paid to the vendor by the purchaser as and when realised. This is a matter for negotiation in the particular circumstances. **17-61**

A Limited Company Practice

Professional practices carried on through limited companies present particular difficulties in valuation, being a hybrid of a private company and a professional practice. It is generally best to value the outgoing partner's shareholding on the same principles as if it were an interest in an unincorporated practice. **17-62**

> **CASE HISTORY: THE SALE OF A SOLE PRACTICE**
>
> A sole practitioner with a substantial practice in a city died after a prolonged illness. Certain of the staff promptly set up their own practice and went about trying to attract as many of the former clients as possible.
>
> The executors of the estate threatened immediate legal action to restrain the staff and, in a compromise, the staff agreed to return and the practice was discreetly advertised for sale. The staff were given the option of matching the highest bid. Annual fees at the time were running at about €800,000 a year. On an expected pre-tax profits margin of 30%, potential annual profits were €240,000.
>
> Seven bids were received. Two were for €280,000 and four in the range of €290,000–€380,000. The top bid was €400,000, not matched by the staff, from an existing two-partner practice. The '*new*' practice did not prosper and, following some financial difficulties, merged with another practice. This was because: (a) the purchasers seriously underestimated the fall-off in business following the changeover; and (b) paid too much for it with the consequent inability to service the related borrowings.

Appendix One

Example of a Letter of Confirmation from Directors

EXAMPLE OF A LETTER OF CONFIRMATION FROM DIRECTORS

The Directors
XYZ Engineering Ltd
10 New Street
Anytown

10 February 20xx

Re: The valuation of 28,000 fully paid Ordinary Shares of €1.27 each in XYZ Engineering Ltd as at 30 June 20xx

Dear Sirs

The Directors of XYZ Engineering Ltd will be aware that I have been instructed to complete the above valuation in accordance with Letter of Engagement dated 15 January 20xx.

It is my understanding that, save as already disclosed in writing to me, the Directors are not aware of any event or circumstance that may materially affect the profitability or continuity of XYZ Engineering Ltd, for good or bad, in the foreseeable future.

It is my further understanding that the Directors, to the best of their knowledge and belief, confirm the accuracy and completeness of the provided information and explanations as set out on the attached Schedule.

Please confirm the above by signing and returning this letter. A copy of this letter is enclosed for your files.

Yours faithfully

John Sutton FCA
Sutton & Metcalfe
Chartered Accountants

On behalf of the Directors of XYZ Engineering Ltd I confirm the contents of this letter

_____   _____
Secretary/Director   **Date**

Appendix Two

Examples of Letters of Engagement

LETTERS OF ENGAGEMENT

A valuation arises in a variety of circumstances. The matters to be covered by the Letter of Engagement ("the Letter") will vary with the circumstances of the particular assignment. The purpose of the Letter is to set out the valuer's understanding of the assignment and the basis on which it will be undertaken. It is good practice to have a Letter on file, even for an informal valuation of a small business. For the latter, a short Letter will probably suffice. Examples of Letters of Engagement are included in this Appendix.

A valuation is not necessarily an end in itself. In most circumstances it is a component in a wider issue such as a possible purchase/sale or a grievance, the next stage being the resolution of that issue through negotiations or litigation. It can happen that a valuation in itself becomes the focal point of the dispute, meaning that one of the parties may choose to interpret the valuation as support, or indeed lack of support, on the merits or demerits of the underlying issue. A break up of negotiations and recriminations can ensue. Hence, time and thought when compiling the Letter of Engagement is well spent.

A valuation report may form expert witness evidence in an arbitration or a court hearing, particularly the latter. Valuations are required in a variety of court cases, commonly in family law and shareholders' disputes.

In framing a Letter of Engagement it is useful to understand what is expected of the valuer acting as an expert witness in such circumstances. The following passage from the UK judgment of Stuart-Smith L.J. in *Loveday v. Renton* (1990), referring to the evaluation of an expert witness (in general – not just regarding a valuation), provides a clear description of what is involved in such an evaluation.

> "This involves an examination of the reasons given for his opinions and the extent to which they are supported by the evidence. The Judge also has to decide what weight to attach to a witness's opinion by examining the internal consistency and logic of his evidence; the care with which he has considered the subject and presented his evidence; his precision and accuracy of thought as

demonstrated by his answers; how he responds to searching and informed cross-examination and in particular the extent to which a witness faces up to and accepts the logic of a proposition put in cross-examination or is prepared to concede points that are seen to be correct; the extent to which a witness has conceived an opinion and is reluctant to re-examine it in the light of later evidence, or demonstrates a flexibility of mind which may involve changing or modifying opinions previously held; whether or not a witness is biased or lacks independence...".

Issues for a valuer to address in a Letter of Engagement include the following:

- Establish exactly the instructing party. For example, it may be the directors of the company or one or more of the shareholders. It may be a solicitor, or a client directly, in a legal case. A valuer needs to understand who has the legal capacity to give the necessary instructions and to whom the valuation is to be actually addressed.

- Know why the valuation is being requested. State the reason at the outset in the Letter.

If somebody does not like the valuation, an attempt may be made to dispute the validity of the valuer's appointment in the first place.

- State in the Letter that the valuation will be reasoned or not reasoned. (See **paras 1–03** and **1–04**).

- The basis of valuation. For example, 'Fair Value', 'Open Market Value' or other method of value. Set out in the Letter the underlying definition of the chosen method of value. (See **Chapter 14**.)

These agree the fundamental structures to the valuation.

- Where there is a grievance, acknowledge that, whilst the grievance has given rise to the valuation, the valuation is independent and is not influenced by, or intended as a measure of, that grievance. An exception is where the grievance has allegedly led to a diminution of the value of the shareholding and this diminution requires a measurement in the valuation.

This will avoid misunderstanding. It also shows the independence necessary for expert evidence in court.

APPENDIX TWO: EXAMPLES OF LETTERS OF ENGAGEMENT

- If there is an asset on the balance sheet (such as property or intellectual property) that may be substantially overvalued or undervalued, state in the Letter that it is the intention to obtain (at the client's expense) an independent third-party valuation or advice on the current valuation of the asset. Do not make your own guess on a valuation of the asset.

- State that it is the intention to seek a Letter of Confirmation from the directors regarding foreseeable events and the accuracy and completeness of provided information and explanations. (See **Appendix One**.)

This is to cover circumstances outside of the valuer's knowledge.

LETTER OF ENGAGEMENT A

(A straightforward valuation in non-contested circumstances)

The Directors
XYZ Engineering Ltd
10 New Street
Anytown

15 January 20xx

LETTER OF ENGAGEMENT

Re: The valuation of 28,000 fully paid Ordinary Shares of €1.27 each ("the shareholding") in XYZ Engineering Ltd ("the Company") as at 30 June 20xx

Dear Sirs

Further to our meeting on 10 January 20xx, I write to confirm my understanding re the above valuation and the terms of engagement. I understand that an independent valuation is required in accordance with the circumstances set out below.

1. The above shareholding is held by the Estate of David Jones, deceased, a former Director of XYZ Engineering Ltd, and comprises 28% of the issued Ordinary Share Capital of the Company.
2. I understand that the remaining 72% of the issued Ordinary Share Capital is held as follows:

John Jones, Executive Director, (brother of the deceased)	24%
William Fitzpatrick, Non-executive Director	35%
Beta Securities Ltd	13%

There are no other classes of share capital in the Company.

3. A copy of the Memorandum and Articles of Association dated 4 December 19xx has been provided. The Articles do not contain a basis of valuation for the transfer of shares in the Company.

4. There is no shareholders' agreement.

5. The date of valuation is 30 June 20xx.

6. It is my understanding that the shareholding being valued is not held in trust or subject to any lien, agreement or option as to its transfer to any party. It is my further understanding that the same position applies to the other shareholdings listed at para 2 above.

7. There is no designated purchaser for the purpose of this valuation. However, it is understood that the shareholding will be offered pro-rata to the other shareholders, and pro-rata again if a shareholder (or shareholders) does not wish to purchase any or all of the pro-rata shareholding. The valuation will not include the possibility of a special purchaser, should a purchaser exist, being willing to pay a higher price than that shown in the valuation.

8. The valuation is to be carried out at 'fair value'. 'Fair value' for this purpose is defined as the amount at which the shareholding could be bought or sold between willing parties. The essence of the 'fair value' concept is the desire to be equitable to both parties. This concept assumes that a buyer is unable to obtain the lowest price and that a seller is unable to obtain the highest price.

9. I will be relying on the information and explanations provided to me by the Directors and management of the company. This will include a review of the audited financial statements for the immediate past three financial years, together with such other information and explanations as I deem necessary to carry out the valuation. In accordance with normal practice, prior to submitting my valuation, I will seek your written confirmation as to the accuracy and completeness of the information and explanations provided, to the best of your knowledge and belief, and that, save as disclosed, the Directors are not aware of any event or circumstance that may materially affect the profitability or continuity, for good or bad, of the Company in the foreseeable future.

10. The valuation is solely for the purpose stated herein and should not be relied upon for any other purpose. With the exception of the Directors and the shareholders in the company, including the Representatives of the Estate of the late David Jones, the valuation may not be provided to any third party without my prior written consent. In no event, regardless of whether consent has been provided,

APPENDIX TWO: EXAMPLES OF LETTERS OF ENGAGEMENT

shall I assume any responsibility to any third party to which the valuation is disclosed or otherwise made available.

11. Whilst my work will involve an analysis of financial and related information, my engagement does not include an audit or independent verification process as to the completeness and accuracy of the information so provided.

12. The valuation of businesses and shares is not a precise science and will, of necessity, be subjective and dependent on the exercise of individual judgement. My valuation will take the form of a concise report. This report will comprise a short summary as to the circumstances of the valuation, a schedule of the information and explanations relied on for the purpose of the valuation, and an amount stated as being my opinion as to the 'fair value' of the shareholding.

13. The costs of the valuation will depend on time spent charged at an hourly rate of €xxx, plus any outlays, and VAT at the rate of xx%. Based on my understanding of the circumstances, I would expect the costs of the valuation to be in the range of estimated €xxxx to €xxxx. This excludes outlays and VAT. Should actual time significantly exceed this range of estimates through factors that could not have been reasonably foreseen at the outset, I will discuss same with you once such circumstance becomes apparent. An invoice will be issued to the Company on completion of my valuation. The valuation report will be issued following payment of the invoice.

Please sign and return the enclosed duplicate of this letter as confirmation that you accept the terms set out in this Letter of Engagement.

Yours faithfully

John Sutton FCA
Sutton & Metcalfe
Chartered Accountants

LETTER OF ENGAGEMENT B

(A valuation in contested circumstances)

Mr Colin Porter
20 Old Street
Anytown

15 January 20xx

LETTER OF ENGAGEMENT

Re: The valuation of 24,250 fully paid Ordinary Shares of €1.27 each ("the shareholding") in Dublin Technics Ltd ("the Company") as at 30 June 20xx and a related valuation of a one-third shareholding in the Company as at 30 June 20xx

Dear Mr Porter

Further to our meeting on 10 January 20xx, I write to confirm my understanding re the above valuation and the terms of engagement. Ms Marie Young of MacArdle & Young, Solicitors, acting on your behalf, also attended the foregoing meeting. For the sake of good order as agreed at our meeting I am sending a copy of this letter to Ms Young.

1. Please feel free to discuss any aspect of this letter with Ms Young and to obtain any advice thereon.

2. I understand that an independent valuation is required of the above shareholding as at 30 June 20xx. The shareholding is in your ownership and is not subject to any trust, lien, agreement or option as to transfer to any party. I understand that you are an Executive Director of the Company.

3. The shareholding comprises 20% of the issued Ordinary Share Capital of the Company. I understand that the remaining 80% of the issued Ordinary Share Capital is held as follows:

Declan O'Rourke	40%
James Gallagher	40%

    Both of these gentlemen are Executive Directors of the Company.

4. There are no other classes of share in the Company.

5. I understand that a legal case is being pursued by you against the above two Directors ("the Defendants") on the grounds of alleged oppression under Section 205 of the Companies Act 1963. I understand that the allegations in this case inter alia include the following:

   (1) That the Defendants unfairly and unreasonably excluded you from active and proper participation in the management and financial affairs of the Company.

   (2) That the Defendants have failed to carry out an understood agreement that they would in time transfer sufficient shareholding to you, at favourable value, to ensure that the three Executive Directors would each hold a one-third interest in the Company.

6. I understand that my instructions are to provide independent valuations as follows:

   (1) The value of your 20% shareholding in the Company as at 30 June 20xx.

   (2) The value of a one-third shareholding in the Company, on the assumption that the shareholdings were held as to one-third each at 30 June 20xx.

7. A copy of the Memorandum and Articles of Association dated 4 December 19xx has been provided. The Articles do not contain a basis of valuation for the transfer of shares in the Company.

8. There is no shareholders' agreement. There is to be an assumption in my valuation that such an agreement, favourable to a minority shareholder, would have been completed had the alleged agreement regarding the one-third shareholdings been completed.

9. I am instructed to carry out each of the valuations at para 6 above using two different methods, as follows:

   (1) The proportionate values of 20% and a one-third interest, to the value of the Company in its entirety, without any discount for minority.

   and

APPENDIX TWO: EXAMPLES OF LETTERS OF ENGAGEMENT

 (2) *The value of a 20% shareholding and a one-third interest, at 'fair value'. 'Fair value' for this purpose is defined as the amount at which the shareholding could be bought or sold between willing parties. The essence of the 'fair value' concept is to be equitable to both parties. This concept assumes that a buyer is unable to obtain the lowest price and that a seller is unable to obtain the highest price.*

10. *It is not my role as valuer to say which, if any, of the above methods of valuation is appropriate to the circumstances of the valuation.*

11. *I will be relying on the information and explanations provided to me by you and through 'discovery'. This will include a review of the audited financial statements for the immediate past three financial years, together with such other information and explanations as I deem necessary to carry out the valuation. As you will readily understand, the environment for seeking information and explanations will be hostile and I will be placing reliance on your knowledge and experience as to the completeness and accuracy of the information and explanations as provided.*

12. *In accordance with normal practice, prior to submitting my valuations, I will seek your written confirmation as to the accuracy and completeness of the information and explanations as provided, to the best of your knowledge and belief and that, save as disclosed, that you are not aware of any event or circumstance that may materially affect the profitability or continuity of the Company, for good or bad, in the foreseeable future.*

13. *Whilst our work will involve an analysis of financial and related information, our engagement does not include an audit or independent verification process as to the completeness and accuracy of the information so provided. Any apparent anomalies or unusual features that come to our attention will, however, be discussed with you and, where appropriate, also with your legal advisers.*

14. *The valuation of businesses and shares is not a precise science and will, of necessity, be subjective and dependent on the exercise of individual judgement. My valuations will be completed on an arm's length and independent basis, meaning that the circumstances and details of the case will not be a factor influencing the valuations.*

15. My valuations will take the form of a report. This report will comprise a short summary of the instructions received, the circumstances of the valuation, without commentary thereon, followed by reasoned valuations. The information and explanations relied on for the purpose of the valuations will be set out on schedules accompanying the report. The valuations will not be precise, but will instead be presented in ranges.

16. The valuations are solely for the purpose stated herein and should not be relied on for any other purpose. Save as may be deemed necessary by your legal advisers, the valuations may not be provided to any third party without my prior written consent. In no event, regardless of whether consent has been provided, shall we assume any responsibility to any third party to which the valuations are disclosed or otherwise made available.

17. The costs of the valuations will depend on time spent at an hourly rate of €xxx, plus any outlays and VAT at the rate of xx%. There will be several different stages involved, namely:

    (1) Assembly of the necessary information. This will likely take some time. Much of the information will be available through your own knowledge and files. However, additional information may only come through 'discovery' or third-party sources.

    (2) There will invariably be a number of attendances and correspondences, with yourself and/or your legal advisers, during the process of assembling the necessary information.

    (3) It is likely that the valuations will require several drafts before final valuations. This is normal practice, and enables input as to clarity and completeness. The valuations are, however, independent and solely my responsibility.

    (4) I would expect that the costs of stages (1), (2) and (3) above to be in the range of estimated €xxxx to €xxxx, plus outlays and VAT at xx%. Should the actual time significantly exceed this range through factors that could not reasonably have been foreseen at the outset, I will discuss same with you once such circumstance becomes apparent.

APPENDIX TWO: EXAMPLES OF LETTERS OF ENGAGEMENT

(5) *An invoice will be issued to you on completion of the valuations to the stage of final draft. In the interim, a payment on account of €xxxx is requested on acceptance of this letter, and a second payment on account of €xxxx is requested when the overall time incurred exceeds €xxxx, the final invoice for the remainder of the costs, at that stage, to be paid within 21 days of its issuance.*

(6) *From thereon, there will be monthly billing of time incurred for payment within 21 days. We cannot estimate these costs at this time. The time incurred will likely include such as*

- *Handling correspondences and attendances with legal advisers re the Statement of Claim, Replies to Particulars, and so on.*
- *Probable liaison with accountants acting for the Defendants.*
- *Attendance at the High Court hearing as required, and at possible prior settlement meetings.*

18. *Please sign and return the enclosed duplicate of this letter as confirmation that you accept the terms of engagement set out in this Letter of Engagement.*

Yours sincerely

John Sutton FCA
Sutton Metcalfe
Chartered Accountants

LETTER OF ENGAGEMENT C

(An indicative 'desktop' valuation)

Ms Jane Johnson
Director
Anglo ABC Agencies Ltd
14 Park Estate
Anytown

15 January 20xx

LETTER OF ENGAGEMENT

Re: Share Valuation

Dear Ms Johnson

I refer to your telephone call of today's date requesting an indicative current valuation of a 23% shareholding in Anglo ABC Agencies Ltd ("the Company").

1. I understand that the shareholder involved has had no involvement with the Company for some time and is agreeable to selling his 23% shareholding to the other shareholders.

2. You would like me to provide an indicative value for the shareholding, with a view to enabling the parties to agree a price. I will have no role in these discussions/negotiations. I am not acting as an expert, mediator or arbitrator in providing an indicative valuation.

3. The indicative valuation is for the use of all the shareholders. The indicative valuation may only be used for the intended purpose and may not be disclosed to third parties.

4. I will rely on a review of the Articles of Association and the audited financial statements for the last three years. I will also rely on an assumption, unless informed otherwise, that the Directors are not aware of any event or circumstance that, for good or bad, will materially affect the profitability or continuity of the Company.

5. Please provide a brief history of the Company and its ownership. Copies of any recent brochures, catalogues or similar of the Company's products or services would be of assistance.

6. My indicative valuation will be provided in a short report. The report will comprise a summary of the financial information relied on, followed by a brief reasoned indicative valuation of the shareholding. The valuation will be shown as a range.

7. The cost of the indicative valuation will be €xxxx, plus VAT at xx%. An invoice will be issued when the report is available. I expect that the report will be available within two weeks from instructions to proceed. On receipt of payment the report will be issued.

Instructions to proceed with the indicative valuation will be an acceptance of the terms of this Letter of Engagement.

Yours sincerely

John Sutton FCA
Sutton & Metcalfe
Chartered Accountants

LETTER OF ENGAGEMENT D

(An informal valuation of a modest business. There is no formal Letter of Engagement, instead a simple letter of a proposed approach to valuation.)

Mr Jack Byrne
XYZ Shopfitters Ltd
6 Back Lane
Anytown

15 January 20xx

Re: Possible Retirement/Sale of Business

Dear Mr Byrne

I write following our meeting on 10 January 20xx. I understand that you now wish to retire or at least phase out from the business.

I advise that I draw up a simple explanation/analysis of the business over recent years. This can be circulated on a low-key basis to a few parties, as dictated by yourself, who might be interested in acquiring the business. The potential sale may be made on the basis of working in tandem with you for an agreed period.

The explanation/analysis is not intended as a formal document, or a valuation. Instead, I advise you to wait and see if any expressions of interest ensure before thinking of price and/or any phase out arrangements.

There is no certainty as to attracting a buyer and it may take some time in any event. However, experience suggests that taking a low-key approach may offer the best chance of success.

If you could call me or drop me a note confirming the above, I will then produce a draft of the explanation/analysis for your consideration. The fees for the work can then be discussed. I suggest that you informally advise your solicitor of your intentions.

Yours sincerely

John Sutton FCA
Sutton Metcalfe
Chartered Accountants

Appendix Three

Examples of Valuation Reports

VALUATION REPORT A

(A straightforward valuation in non-contested circumstances)

VALUATION REPORT

The purpose of this Report is to set out a valuation of 28,000 fully paid Ordinary Shares of €1.27 each ("the shareholding") in XYZ Engineering Ltd ("the Company") as at 30 June 20xx.

1. *This valuation is in accordance with the Letter of Engagement dated 15 January 20xx and the Letter should be treated as part of this valuation. For the sake of good order, a copy of the Letter of Engagement is attached as an appendix to this Report.*

   [See Letter of Engagement A, above in **Appendix One**]

2. *The valuation is to be carried out at 'fair value'. 'Fair value' for this purpose is defined as the amount at which the shareholding could be bought or sold between willing parties. The essence of the 'fair value' concept is the desire to be equitable to both parties. The concept assumes that a buyer is unable to obtain the lowest price and that a seller is unable to obtain the highest price.*

3. *A schedule of information that I have relied on is set out as an appendix to this Report. My engagement does not include an audit or independent verification process as to the completeness and accuracy of the information so provided.*

4. *The trading results for the latest three financial years can be summarised as follows:*

Year ended 30 June	*20xx*	*20xx*	*20xx*
(Euro thousands)			
Sales	____	____	____
Gross Profit (GP)			
GP as % of sales	____	____	____
Directors' Remuneration			
Interest paid			

Depreciation
Other expenses

Total expenses   _____   _____   _____
Pre-tax profits
Tax on profits
                                    _____   _____   _____
Net-of-tax profits (*)

(*) excluding an exceptional profit of € xxxxx on disposal of a property in the year 20xx

5. *I have not found it necessary to make any adjustment to the trading results for unusual and/or non-recurring sales or expenses, save for the exceptional profit on the disposal of a property in the year 20xx. The balance sheet at 30 June 20xx does not have any factors/features that would influence the valuation.*

6. *The Directors have provided a Letter of Confirmation dated 10 February 20xx stating that they are not aware of any event or circumstance that might materially affect the profitability or continuity, for good or bad, of the Company in the foreseeable future. A copy of the Letter is attached to this Report.*

   [An example of a Letter of Confirmation from Directors is on page 131.]

7. *The trading results set out at para 4 above show a reasonably consistent level of annual net-of-tax profits. On the assumption of continuity in this regard, and including an increase of 8% regarding expectations on trading in the current financial year ending 30 June 20xx, I have taken annual future maintainable net-of-tax profits as €xxxx.*

APPENDIX THREE: EXAMPLES OF VALUATION REPORTS

8. In the opinion of the author, a multiple of six is appropriate to the circumstances of the Company. Hence the valuation of the Company in its entirety is:

$$€xxxxxxx \times 6 = €xxxxxxxx$$

9. The shareholding comprises 28% of the issued Ordinary Share Capital of the Company. In the normal course, the minority discount as commonly applied to such a level of shareholding is 35% to 40%.

10. The other shareholdings in the Company are:

    35%   24%   13%

11. The 28% is an influential minority shareholding in the context of the spread of the other shareholdings in the Company. Combined with either the 35% or 24% shareholding, it represents part of a possible majority interest of 63% or 52% respectively.

12. In my opinion, on the concept of 'fair value' as applied in these circumstances, a lesser minority discount of 20% should be applied. The calculation is as follows:

Valuation of entire company		€xxxxxxx
(see para 8 above)		
€xxxxxxx × 28%	=	€xxxxxxx
Deduct minority discount @ 20%	=	(€xxxxxx)
Valuation	=	€xxxxxxx

13. In my opinion, the valuation of 28,000 fully paid Ordinary Shares of €1.27 each in XYZ Engineering Ltd as at 30 June 20xx is €xxxxxx.

Sutton & Metcalfe   **John Sutton FCA**
Chartered Accountants   **12 February 20xx**

VALUATION REPORT B

(A valuation in contested circumstances)

VALUATION REPORT

The purpose of this Report is to set out a valuation of 24,250 fully paid Ordinary Shares of €1.27 each ("the shareholding") in Dublin Technics Ltd ("the Company") as at 30 June 20xx and a related valuation of a one-third shareholding in the Company as at 30 June 20xx.

1. *This valuation is in accordance with the Letter of Engagement dated 15 January 20xx and the Letter should be treated as part of this valuation. For the sake of good order, a copy of the Letter of Engagement is attached as an appendix to this Report.*

   [See Letter of Engagement B on page 143.]

2. *The valuation is to be carried out using two different methods, as follows:*

   (1) *The proportionate values of 20%, and of a one-third interest, to the value of the Company in its entirety, without any discount for minority.*

   and

   (2) *The value of 20% shareholding and a one-third interest, at 'fair value'. 'Fair value' for this purpose is defined as the amount at which the shareholding could be bought or sold between willing parties. The essence of the 'fair value' concept is to be equitable to both parties. This concept assumes that a buyer is unable to obtain the lowest price and that a seller is unable to obtain the highest price.*

3. *A schedule of information relied on is set out as an appendix to this Report. My engagement does not include an audit or independent verification process as to the completeness and accuracy of the information so provided.*

4. *A summary of the trading results, as shown in the audited accounts for the latest three financial years, is set out in an appendix to this Report. As shown in the summary, a number of accounting*

THE VALUATION OF BUSINESSES AND SHARES

adjustments have been made to the results to reflect unusual and/or non-recurring items as identified by Mr Porter, the person requesting this valuation. The balance sheet at 30 June 20xx does not have any factors/features that would influence the valuation.

5. The adjusted net-of-tax profits can be summarised as follows:

Year ended 30 June   20xx   20xx   20xx

(Euro thousands)

Adjusted net-of-tax profits

6. The trading results, as adjusted, show an erratic pattern of annual net-of-tax profits. Nevertheless, it is the advice of Mr Porter, on which I have relied, that the net-of-tax profits for the latest financial year ended 30 June 20xx may reasonably be taken as representative of annual future maintainable net-of-profits. These net-of-tax profits are €xxxxxx.

7. It is uncertain that a purchaser could readily be found for what is a narrowly focused specialist company, heavily dependent on the technical expertise of the two Executive Directors. The Company is largely a 'stand-alone' business that would not likely provide synergies if merged with another similar business.

8. Primarily for these reasons, in my opinion a multiple of four-to-five times the annual future maintainable net-of-tax profits is appropriate to the circumstances of the Company. Hence the valuation of the company in its entirety is in the range of:

$$€xxxxxxx \times 4 = €xxxxxxxx$$
$$€xxxxxxx \times 5 = €xxxxxxxx$$

9. Accordingly the valuations of a 20% shareholding, and of a one-third interest, without discount for minority, are as follows:

	Multiple of 4	Multiple of 5
Valuation of entire company	_____	_____
20% of above valuation =		
One-third of above valuation =		

APPENDIX THREE: EXAMPLES OF VALUATION REPORTS

10. In the normal course, the minority discount as commonly applied to a shareholding of 20% is 50% to 70% and, to a shareholding of one-third, 35% to 40%.

11. The other shareholdings in the company are two shareholdings of 40%, or two shareholdings of one-third each as relevant to the instructions set out in the Letter of Engagement dated 15 January 20xx.

12. In either of the above circumstances, the respective shareholdings of 20% and one-third may be seen as an influential minority. Combined with one of the other shareholdings, either of the foregoing represents part of a possible majority interest.

13. Accordingly, the concept of 'fair value' as applied in these circumstances is such that, in my opinion, a lesser minority discount of 25% should be applied. The calculations of valuations are as follows:

(Euro)		*Multiple of 4*	*Multiple of 5*
Valuation of entire company			
20% of above valuation	=		
(Deduct 25% minority discount)	=	( )	( )
Valuation of 20% shareholding	=		
One-third of above valuation	=		
(Deduct 25% minority discount)	=	( )	( )
Valuation of one-third shareholding	=		

14. In my opinion, in accordance with the instructions received as per Letter of Engagement dated 15 January 20xx, the valuations are as follows:

Valuation of 24,250 fully paid Ordinary Shares of €1.27 each in Dublin Technics Ltd at 30 June 20xx:

A range of €xxxxxxx to €xxxxxxx

Valuation of a one-third shareholding in Dublin Technics Ltd at 30 June 20xx:

A range of €xxxxxxx to €xxxxxxx

Sutton & Metcalfe **John Sutton FCA**
Chartered Accountants **12 February 20xx**

VALUATION REPORT C

(An indicative 'desktop' valuation)

VALUATION REPORT

The purpose of this Report is to set out an indicative current valuation of a 23% shareholding in Anglo ABC Agencies Ltd ("the Company").

1. *This indicative valuation is in accordance with the Letter of Engagement dated 15 January 20xx and the Letter should be treated as part of this valuation. For the sake of good order, a copy of the Letter of Engagement is attached as an appendix to this Report.*

   [See Letter of Engagement C above in **Appendix Two**.]

2. *The owner of the 23% shareholding has had no involvement with the Company for some time and is agreeable to selling his interest to the other shareholders. I understand that all of the other shareholders have full knowledge of the trading and financial circumstances of the Company.*

3. *The information that I have relied on for my valuation is set out in an appendix to this Report.*

4. *A brief summary of the Company's trading results for the latest three financial years is attached as an appendix to this Report. I also show in the summary a straightforward analysis/calculation of future annual net-of-tax maintainable profits. This analysis/calculation has been discussed with all of the shareholders and has been agreed as a reasonable estimate of future annual net-of-tax maintainable profits.*

5. *Should the entire Company be currently placed for sale in the marketplace, I would expect it to attract a purchaser willing to pay a price of between a multiple of five-to-seven times the future annual net-of-tax maintainable profits.*

6. This would give a valuation for the entire Company in the range of:

   €xxxxxxx x 5   =   €xxxxxxx

   €xxxxxxx x 7   =   €xxxxxxx

7. The valuation of the 23% shareholding is to be carried out at 'fair value'. 'Fair value' for this purpose is defined as the amount at which the shareholding could be bought or sold between willing parties. The essence of the 'fair value' concept is to be equitable to both parties. This concept assumes that a buyer is unable to obtain the lowest price and that a seller is unable to obtain the highest price.

8. The accepted minority discount for a 23% shareholding, on the assumption that the shareholdings is non-influential, would be in the range of 50% to 70% applied to the value of the Company in its entirety. In my opinion, the appropriate minority discount as relevant to the concept of 'fair value', in the circumstances of this valuation, is in the range of 20% to 30%.

9. Accordingly, in my opinion, the range of indicative valuations is as follows:

(Euro)		Multiple of 5	Multiple of 7
Valuation of entire Company (para 6 above)		_____	_____
(1) 23% of above valuation	=		
(Deduct minority discount at 20%)	=	( )	( )
Valuation	=		
(2) 23% of above valuation	=		
(Deduct minority discount at 20%)	=	( )	( )
Valuation	=		

Sutton & Metcalfe **John Sutton FCA**
Chartered Accountants **12 February 20xx**

Appendix Four

Revenue Guidelines on Share Valuation

CAPITAL ACQUISITION TAX MANUAL

Part 21 – Valuation of Unquoted Shares

Revision Date: 22nd September 2009

Table of Contents

Part 21 – Valuation of Unquoted Shares 167
Table of Contents 167
Capital Acquisitions Tax 168
21. Part 21 – Valuation of Unquoted Shares 168
   21.1. Introduction 168
   21.2. Aims of Valuation 168
   21.3. Valuation of Shares 168
   21.4. Valuation Based on Earnings 168
   21.5. Valuation Based on Assets 170
   21.6. Valuations Based on Turnover Fees or Commissions 170
   21.7. Control of a Company 170
   21.8. Definition of Control 170
   21.9. Explanatory Note on Relatives 171
   21.10. Effects of Control 171
   21.11. Different Classes of Shares 171
   21.12. Size of Shareholding 173
   21.13. Majority Shareholding/Influential Minority Shareholding .. 173
      21.13.1. Holdings of 50% and above 173
      21.13.2. Minority Shareholding 173
   21.14. Stages in Valuation 174

Capital Acquisitions Tax

21. Part 21 – Valuation of Unquoted Shares

21.1. Introduction

Valuation of unquoted shares is often said to be more of an art than a science.

Various methods of valuation have been put forward over the years.

As part of its audit function, Revenue values unquoted shares which are held in private or public companies which are not listed/quoted on a Stock Exchange.

21.2. Aims of Valuation

- To ensure that valuations submitted in respect of unquoted shares reflect the open market values.
- To deter evasion and avoidance by detecting under-valuations and taking appropriate action.

21.3. Valuation of Shares

Valuation is not an exact science. The value of a shareholding depends on many factors - the nature/size of the shareholding passing, profitability of the business and its future prospects in the marketplace at the time of the transaction.

When valuing shares in unquoted companies for tax purposes, the shares passing must be valued on the basis of a hypothetical sale in a hypothetical open market between a hypothetical willing vendor and a hypothetical willing purchaser.

Depending on the nature of the company's business, different valuation methodologies may be employed.

21.4. Valuation Based on Earnings

Trading and manufacturing companies are normally valued on the basis of a multiple of their maintainable after-tax

APPENDIX FOUR: REVENUE GUIDELINES ON SHARE VALUATION

profits. This multiple is known as the price earnings ratio. The multiple used may vary depending on the particular industry in which the company is engaged.

The appropriate multiple is normally selected by reference to a quoted company/companies in the same industry. Financial information in respect of quoted companies is published regularly in the national newspapers. The results of these companies are analysed in relation to their trading performance and the prices at which their shares are sold are expressed as a multiple of their after-tax profits.

When a suitable quoted company has been identified, the normal practice is to use the multiple of after-tax profits appropriate to that quoted company, less a discount of 20% to compensate for the lack of access to the market which a quote on the stock exchange provides, i.e.

If the multiple of after-tax profits for the quoted company is 10, the appropriate multiple for an unquoted company would be 8, but this may be further reduced if the unquoted company is a relatively small one.

> **Example**
>
> Company's after-tax profits
>
> €250,000
> Price Earnings Ratio (say)
> 8
> Value of Company
>
> €2,000,000

This is known as the Earnings method of valuation and most companies are valued on this basis.

If a company has retained profits or assets of any sort not immediately required for the purpose of its trade, the value of all such assets would normally be added to the company's earnings value.

21.5. Valuation Based on Assets

Investment holding or property holding companies are normally valued on the basis of their net assets value. The values shown on the Balance Sheet for property or investments may not normally represent their true value. It is generally necessary therefore to obtain up-to-date values as at valuation date for these assets and substitute market value for book value on the Balance Sheet when carrying out a valuation.

21.6. Valuations Based on Turnover Fees or Commissions

Companies which own or operate Licensed Premises or Restaurants or whose business is in the services sector, such as Insurance Brokers, Quantity Surveyors, Architectural Practices, Consulting Engineers, Legal etc. are normally valued on the basis of a multiple of their turnover, fees or commissions.

21.7. Control of a Company

Where a company is a "company controlled by the donee or successor", Section 27 of the Capital Acquisitions Tax Consolidation Act 2003 provides that the shares must be valued on the basis that the owner is deemed to have control of the company. The combined shareholdings of the donee or successor and his or her relatives (and of the trustees of any settlement whose objects include the donee or successor or relatives of the donee or successor) are taken into account both for the purpose of ascertaining whether or not the company is controlled and for the purpose of measuring the extent of the control.

21.8. Definition of Control

Control under Section 27 is defined and covers voting control (direct or indirect). Control is recognised as—

- the capacity to exercise the power of a board of directors,
- the right to receive more than one half of total dividends,
- an interest in the shares of the company representing one half or more of the total nominal value of the shares of the company,

- the powers of a board of directors of the company,
- powers of a governing director of the company,
- the power to nominate a majority of the directors of the company or a governing director thereof,
- the power to veto the appointment of a director of the company or powers of a like nature.

21.9. Explanatory Note on Relatives

"Relative of the donee or successor" as defined by Section 2(4) of the Capital Acquisitions Tax Consolidation Act 2003 includes—

a) the spouse;

b) the mother, father, children, uncles and aunts;

c) brothers, sisters, nephews, nieces, grandchildren, great-grandchildren, first cousins and their children;

d) spouses of those mentioned at (b) and (c);

e) grandparents.

21.10. Effects of Control

Under these provisions, shares in companies that are owned by an individual or by relatives of an individual are to be valued as a proportionate part of the entire shareholding in the company held by that individual and relatives of that individual.

21.11. Different Classes of Shares

Section 27 also provides that, where different classes of shares exist, each class of share must be valued in the light of the advantages and disadvantages that attach to them.

Valuation examples of controlled companies illustrating the effect where there are more than one class of shares with different rights.

Controlled Company .... Issued Share Capital 100 Ordinary €1.00 shares all shares pari passu.

Company worth   €20,000

Value of 1 share $\dfrac{€20.000 \times 1}{100}$

= €200 per share

Controlled Company .... Issued Share Capital 80 Ordinary €1.00 shares and 20 A Ordinary Voting Shares. Other than voting rights, all shares pari passu. (Voting shares are allocated a premium value equivalent to 15% of the value of the company to reflect the power which attaches to them.)

Company worth   €20,000

A shares voting premium   €3,000

Balance for distribution between voting and non-voting shares €17,000

Valuation of A Ordinary Shares

$\dfrac{€17,000 \times 80}{100}$ = $\dfrac{€13,600}{80}$ = €170 per Ordinary Share

Value of A Ordinary Shares

$\dfrac{€17,000 \times 20}{100}$ + Voting Premium €3,000

Value of one A Ordinary Voting Shares

$\dfrac{€170 \times 20 + \text{Voting Premium } €3,000}{20}$ = €170 + €150 + €320 per share

APPENDIX FOUR: REVENUE GUIDELINES ON SHARE VALUATION

Difference in value therefore:

Ordinary Non-Voting Shares €170 per share

Voting A Ordinary Shares €320 per share

Value of Voting Rights therefore = €150 per share.

21.12. Size of Shareholding

The size of the shareholding passing reflects the amount of control that a shareholder can exercise on the running of a company and the value of a particular shareholding is normally discounted to reflect the advantages/disadvantages attaching to same.

A 75% – 100% shareholder has full control over all matters affecting the company, including the power to wind it up.

A 51% – 74% shareholder has the power (control) to do all things except wind the company up.

A 50% shareholder needs the support of another shareholder to pass an ordinary resolution.

21.13. Majority Shareholding/Influential Minority Shareholding

21.13.1. Holdings of 50% and above

Value by reference to the value of the whole company less a suitable discount, e.g.

75%+	Nil discount or perhaps 5% at most
50%+ 1	10 – 15%
50%	20 – 30%
25%+ 1	35 – 40%

21.13.2. Minority Shareholding

Up to 25% – value by reference to dividends if a realistic level of dividend is being paid. If no dividend, look at discounted earnings with a discount range of 50% – 70%, as these are influential minority holdings.

21.14. Stages in Valuation

1. Calculate the value of the entire company.
2. Value the shareholding passing.
3. Discount gross value to reflect size of shareholding passing, taking account of the deemed control provisions of Section 27 of the Capital Acquisitions Tax Consolidation Act 2003.

Form Q7

CAPITAL ACQUISITIONS TAX
VALUATION OF UNQUOTED SHARES

for Official use only

PART 1 — GENERAL INFORMATION

Disperser's RSI No.
Agent's Ref.
Name of company
Business location
Date of incorporation
Nature of business
Issued share capital — Ords: | Prefs: | Others:
Shares to be valued — Ords: | Prefs: | Others:
Valuation date | Consideration paid per share | Value submitted per share

PART 2 — CONTROLLED COMPANIES

Was the company controlled by the donee or successor within the meaning of Section 16 of the Capital Acquisitions Tax Act 1976, Section 107 (a) Finance Act, 1984 or Section 104(a) Finance Act, 1986 (after taking the gift or inheritance) on the date of the gift or inheritance? (✓)   Yes ☐   No ☐
For explanatory notes on control/relatives see overleaf.

Detail below precisely the relationship of the donee/successor to the other shareholders (use a separate sheet if necessary).
Note — if at the valuation date any shareholder held shares as a nominee or trustee for the donee/successor this should be indicated.

Shareholder	No. and class of shares held	Rights attaching to each class of share	Relationship of shareholder to donee or successor

PART 3 — VALUATION DETAILS

Indicate the basis of valuation for the shares being transferred: (✓)   Earnings ☐;   Assets ☐;   Dividend yield ☐;   Hybrid ☐;   Other ☐

Provide full sets of the company's audited accounts for the 3 years prior to the valuation date and set out the information requested below regarding the earnings or assets values, depending on the method of valuation used.

VALUATION BASED ON EARNINGS (I.E. PROFITS)
Set out the following information from the relevant audited accounts:

Turnover €
Pre-tax profits €
After tax profits €
The multiple of earnings used in your calculation
The earnings valuation of the company €
The earnings value per share €
Discount %
Value per share €

VALUATION BASED ON ASSETS
The market value of all property and investments held by the company and its subsidiaries or associate companies must be substituted for their book values when calculating the adjusted assets value of the company.

Book assets value €
State the increase which arises on substituting market value for net book value of any property held €
State the increase which arises on substituting market value for net book value of investments held €
Adjusted assets value €
After tax profits earned since date of last accounts €
Revised net assets value of the company €
Net assets value per share €   Discount %   Value per share €

VALUATION BASED ON DIVIDEND YIELD
If this method is used state on a separate sheet the basis on which it is calculated

---

If the valuation is based on a methodology other than that outlined above or on a combination (hybrid method) of earnings/assets/dividend yield, outline on a separate sheet how the valuation was arrived at.

Form Q7

PART 4 PRIOR SALES

Provide details of prior sales of shares in the company within the previous 3 years

No. of shares sold	Price paid per share	Relationship between the parties

It should be noted that

- the informaton supplied may be sufficient to allow valuation proceed without further query.
- in the event that the value offered is found to be understated, appropriate surcharges are provided for under Section 79 of the Finance Act, 1989 and will be imposed.
- the acceptance of a value for CAT purposes is entirely without prejudice to any valuation of shares in the same company for any other Revenue purposes

Transactions are subject to audit. Penalties may be incurred where incorrect information is given.

PART 5 CERTIFICATE

I certify that the information given above is true and complete and that, in my opinion, the value offered represents the full market value of the shares transferred.

Signed _____ Date _____

Accountable Person/Agent

DOCUMENTS TO ACCOMPANY THIS FORM

Checklist (✓)

☐ Audited accounts for the 3 years preceding the valuation date for the company and its subsidiaries or associate companies. (Consolidated accounts if available should be supplied).

☐ If more than one class of share exists at the valuation date kindly furnish a copy of the memo and articles of association of the company and all amendments thereto since the date of incorporation outlining rights attaching to each class of share.

EXPLANATORY NOTES ON CONTROL AND RELATIVES

Where a company is a "company controlled by the donee or successor", Secton 16 of the Capital Acquisitions Tax Act, 1976 provides that the shares must be valued on the basis that the owner is deemed to have control of the company. The combined shareholdings of the donee or successor and his or her relatives (and of the trustees of any settlement whose objects include the donee or successor or relatives of the donee or successor) are taken into account both for the purpose of ascertaining whether or not the company is controlled and for the purpose of measuring the extent of the control.

Control under Section 16 is defined and covers voting control (direct or indirect).

Control is recognised as —

- the capacity to exercise the power of a board of directors,
- the right to receive more than one half of total dividends,
- an interest in the shares of the company representing one half or more of the total nominal value of the shares of the company,
- the powers of a board of directors of the company,
- powers of a governing director of the company,
- the power to nominate a majority of the directors of the company or a governing director thereof,
- the power to veto the appointment of a director of the company or powers of a like nature.

"Relative of the donee or successor" as defined by Section 2(4) of the Capital Acquisitions Tax Act, 1976 includes —

(a) the spouse;
(b) the mother, father, children, uncles and aunts;
(c) brothers, sisters, nephews, nieces, grandchildren, great-grandchildren, first cousins and their children;
(d) spouses of those mentioned at (b) and (c);
(e) grandparents.

Revenue

Appendix Five

The Partnership Act 1890

Partnership Act, 1890.*

[53 & 54 Vict.]   [Ch. **39.**]

ARRANGEMENT OF SECTIONS.

A.D. 1890.

Nature of Partnership.

Section.
1. Definition of partnership.
2. Rules for determining existence of partnership.
3. Postponement of rights of person lending or selling in consideration of share of profits in case of insolvency.
4. Meaning of firm.

Relations of Partners to persons dealing with them.
5. Power of partner to bind the firm.
6. Partners bound by acts on behalf of firm.
7. Partner using credit of firm for private purposes.
8. Effect of notice that firm will not be bound by acts of partner.
9. Liability of partners.
10. Liability of the firm for wrongs.
11. Misapplication of money or property received for or in custody of the firm.
12. Liability for wrongs joint and several.
13. Improper employment of trust-property for partnership purposes.
14. Persons liable by "holding out."
15. Admissions and representations of partners.
16. Notice to acting partner to be notice to the firm.
17. Liabilities of incoming and outgoing partners.
18. Revocation of continuing guaranty by change in firm.

---

*Crown copyright, reproduced with the permission of the Controller of Her Majesty's Stationery Office.

Relations of Partners to one another.
19. Variation by consent of terms of partnership.
20. Partnership property.
21. Property bought with partnership money.
22. Conversion into personal estate of land held as partnership property.
23. Procedure against partnership property for a partner's separate judgment debt.
24. Rules as to interests and duties of partners subject to special agreement.
25. Expulsion of partner.
26. Retirement from partnership at will.
27. Where partnership for term is continued over, continuance on old terms presumed.
28. Duty of partners to render accounts, &c.
29. Accountability of partners for private profits.
30. Duty of partner not to compete with firm.
31. Rights of assignee of share in partnership.

Dissolution of Partnership, and its consequences.
32. Dissolution by expiration or notice.
33. Dissolution by bankruptcy, death, or charge.
34. Dissolution by illegality of partnership.
35. Dissolution by the Court.
36. Rights of persons dealing with firm against apparent members of firm.
37. Right of partners to notify dissolution.
38. Continuing authority of partners for purposes of winding up.
39. Rights of partners as to application of partnership property.
40. Apportioning of premium where partnership prematurely dissolved.
41. Rights where partnership dissolved for fraud or misrepresentation.
42. Right of outgoing partner in certain cases to share profits made after dissolution.

APPENDIX FIVE: THE PARTNERSHIP ACT 1890

43. Retiring or deceased partner's share to be a debt.
44. Rule for distribution of assets on final settlement of accounts.

Supplemental.

45. Definitions of "court" and "business."
46. Saving for rules of equity and common law.
47. Provision as to bankruptcy in Scotland.
48. Repeal.
49. Commencement of Act.
50. Short title.
    SCHEDULE

An Act to declare and amend the Law of Partnership. [14th August 1890.]

BE it enacted by the Queen's most Excellent Majesty, by and with the advice and consent of the Lords Spiritual and Temporal, and Commons, in this present Parliament assembled, and by the authority of the same, as follows:-

Nature of Partnership.

1.–(1) Partnership is the relation which subsists between persons carrying on a business in common with a view of profit. Definition of partnership.

(2) But the relation between members of any company or association which is–
   (a) Registered as a company under the Companies Act, 1862, or any other Act of Parliament for the time being in force and relating to the registration of joint stock companies; or 25 & 26 Vict. c. 89.
   (b) Formed or incorporated by or in pursuance of any other Act of Parliament or letters patent, or Royal Charter; or
   (c) A company engaged in working mines within and subject to the jurisdiction of the Stannaries:

is not a partnership within the meaning of this Act.

2. In determining whether a partnership does or does not exist, regard shall be had to the following rules:

(1) Joint tenancy, tenancy in common, joint property, common property, or part ownership does not of itself create a partnership as to any thing so held or owned, whether the tenants or owners do or do not share any profits made by the use thereof.

(2) The sharing of gross returns does not of itself create a partnership, whether the persons sharing such returns have or have not a joint or common right or interest in any property from which or from the use of which the returns are derived.

(3) The receipt by a person of a share of the profits of a business is *primâ facie* evidence that he is a partner in the business, but the receipt of such a share, or of a payment contingent on or varying with the profits of a business, does not of itself make him a partner in the business; and in particular–

(*a*) The receipt by a person of a debt or other liquidated amount by instalments, or otherwise out of the accruing profits of a business does not of itself make him a partner in the business or liable as such:

(*b*) A contract for the remuneration of a servant or agent of a person engaged in a business by a share of the profits of the business does not of itself make the servant or agent a partner in the business or liable as such:

(*c*) A person being the widow or child of a deceased partner, and receiving by way of annuity a portion of the profits made in the business in which the deceased person was a partner, is not by reason only of such receipt a partner in the business or liable as such:

(*d*) The advance of money by way of loan to a person engaged or about to engage in any business on a contract with that person that the lender shall receive a rate of interest varying with the profits, or shall receive a share of the profits arising from carrying on the business, does not of itself make the lender a partner with the person or persons carrying on the business or liable as such. Provided that the contract is in writing, and signed by or on behalf of all the parties thereto:

(*e*) A person receiving by way of annuity or otherwise a portion of the profits of a business in consideration of the sale by him of the goodwill of the business is not by reason only of such receipt a partner in the business or liable as such.

3. In the event of any person to whom money has been advanced by way of loan upon such a contract as is mentioned in the last foregoing section, or of any buyer of a goodwill in consideration of a share of the profits of the business, being adjudged a bankrupt, entering into an arrangement to pay his creditors less than twenty shillings in the pound, or dying in insolvent circumstances, the lender of the loan shall not be entitled to recover anything in respect of his loan, and the seller of the goodwill shall not be entitled to recover anything in respect of the share of profits contracted for, until the claims of the other creditors of the borrower or buyer for valuable consideration in money or money's worth have been satisfied. *Postponement of rights of person lending or selling in consideration of share of profits in case of insolvency.*

Meaning of firm.

4.-(l) Persons who have entered into partnership with one another are for the purposes of this Act called collectively a firm, and the name under which their business is carried on is called the firm-name.

(2) In Scotland a firm is a legal person distinct from the partners of whom it is composed, but an individual partner may be charged on a decree or diligence directed against the firm, and on payment of the debts is entitled to relief *pro ratâ* from the firm and its other members.

Relations of Partners to persons dealing with them.

Power of partner to bind the firm.

5. Every partner is an agent of the firm and his other partners for the purpose of the business of the partnership; and the acts of every partner who does any act for carrying on in the usual way business of the kind carried on by the firm of which he is a member bind the firm and his partners, unless the partner so acting has in fact no authority to act for the firm in the particular matter, and the person with whom he is dealing either knows that he has no authority, or does not know or believe him to be a partner.

Partners bound by acts on behalf of firm.

6. An act or instrument relating to the business of the firm and done or executed in the firm-name, or in any other manner showing an intention to bind the firm, by any person thereto authorised, whether a partner or not, is binding on the firm and all the partners.

Provided that this section shall not affect any general rule of law relating to the execution of deeds or negotiable instruments.

Effect of notice that firm will not be bound by acts of partner.

7. Where one partner pledges the credit of the firm for a purpose apparently not connected with the firm's ordinary course of business, the firm is not bound, unless he is in fact specially authorised by the other partners; but this section does not affect any personal liability incurred by an individual partner.

8. If it has been agreed between the partners that any restriction shall be placed on the power of any one or more of them to bind the firm, no act done in contravention of the agreement is binding on the firm with respect to persons having notice of the agreement.

9. Every partner in a firm is liable jointly with the other partners, and in Scotland severally also, for all debts and obligations of the firm incurred while he is a partner; and after his death his estate is also severally liable in a due course of administration for such debts and obligations, so far as they remain unsatisfied, but subject in England or Ireland to the prior payment of his separate debts. *[Liability of partners.]*

10. Where, by any wrongful act or omission of any partner acting in the ordinary course of the business of the firm, or with the authority of his co-partners, loss or injury is caused to any person not being a partner in the firm, or any penalty is incurred, the firm is liable therefor to the same extent as the partner so acting or omitting to act.

11. In the following cases; namely–

(*a*) Where one partner acting within the scope of his apparent authority receives the money or property of a third person and misapplies it; and

(*b*) Where a firm in the course of its business received money or property of a third person, and the money or property so received is misapplied by one or more of the partners while it is in the custody of the firm;

the firm is liable to make good the loss.

12. Every partner is liable jointly with his co-partners and also severally for everything for which the firm while he is a partner therein becomes liable under either of the two last preceding sections. *[Liability for wrongs joint and several.]*

Improper employment of trust-property for partnership purposes.

13. If a partner, being a trustee, improperly employs trust-property in the business or on the account of the partnership, no other partner is liable for the trust-property to the persons beneficially interested therein.

Provided as follows:-

(1) This section shall not affect any liability incurred by any partner by reason of his having notice of a breach of trust; and

(2) Nothing in this section shall prevent trust money from being followed and recovered from the firm if still in its possession or under its control.

Persons liable by "holding out."

14.–(1) Every one who by words spoken or written or by conduct represents himself, or who knowingly suffers himself to be represented, as a partner in a particular firm, is liable as a partner to any one who has on the faith of any such representation given credit to the firm, whether the representation has or has not been made or communicated to the person so giving credit by or with the knowledge of the apparent partner making the representation or suffering it to be made.

(2) Provided that where after a partner's death the partnership business is continued in the old firm-name, the continued use of that name or of the deceased partner's name as part thereof shall not of itself make his executors or administrators estate or effects liable for any partnership debts contracted after his death.

Admissions and representations of partners.

15. An admission or representation made by any partner concerning the partnership affairs, and in the ordinary course of its business, is evidence against the firm.

Notice to acting partner to be notice to the firm.

16. Notice to any partner who habitually acts in the partnership business of any matter relating to partnership affairs operates as notice to the firm, except in the case of a fraud on the firm committed by or with the consent of that partner.

17.–(1) A person who is admitted as a partner into an existing firm does not thereby become liable to the creditors of the firm for anything done before he became a partner.

Liabilities of incoming and outgoing partners.

(2) A partner who retires from a firm does not thereby cease to be liable for partnership debts or obligations incurred before his retirement.

(3) A retiring partner may be discharged from any existing liabilities, by an agreement to that effect between himself and the members of the firm as newly constituted and the creditors, and this agreement may be either express or inferred as a fact from the course of dealing between the creditors and the firm as newly constituted.

18. A continuing guaranty or cautionary obligation given either to a firm or to a third person in respect of the transactions of a firm is, in the absence of agreement to the contrary, revoked as to future transactions by any change in the constitution of the firm to which, or of the firm in respect of the transactions of which, the guaranty or obligation was given.

Revocation of continuing guaranty by change in firm.

Relations of Partners to one another.

19. The mutual rights and duties of partners, whether ascertained by agreement or denned by this Act, may be varied by the consent of all the partners, and such consent may be either express or inferred from a course of dealing.

Variation by consent of terms of partnership.

20.–(l) All property and rights and interests in property originally brought into the partnership stock or acquired, whether by purchase or otherwise, on account of the firm or for the purposes and in the course of the partnership business, are called in this Act partnership property, and must be held and applied by the

Partnership property.

partners exclusively for the purposes of the partnership and in accordance with the partnership agreement.

(2) Provided that the legal estate or interest in any land, or in Scotland the title to and interest in any heritable estate, which belongs to the partnership shall devolve according to the nature and tenure thereof, and the general rules of law thereto applicable, but in trust, so far as necessary, for the persons beneficially interested in the land under this section.

(3) Where co-owners of an estate or interest in any land, or in Scotland of any heritable estate, not being itself partnership property, are partners as to profits made by the use of that land or estate, and purchase other land or estate out of the profits to be used in like manner, the land or estate so purchased belongs to them, in the absence of an agreement to the contrary, not as partners but as co-owners for the same respective estates and interests as are held by them in the land or estate first mentioned at the date of the purchase.

Property bought with partnership money.

21. Unless the contrary intention appears, property bought with money belonging to the firm is deemed to have been bought on account of the firm.

Conversion into personal estate of land held as partnership property.

22. Where land or any heritable interest therein has become partnership property, it shall, unless the contrary intention appears, be treated as between the partners (including the representatives of a deceased partner), and also as between the heirs of a deceased partner and his executors or administrators, as personal or moveable and not real or heritable estate.

Procedure against partnership property for a partner's separate judgment debt.

23.—(1) After the commencement of this Act a writ of execution shall not issue against any partnership property except on a judgment against the firm.

(2) The High Court, or a judge thereof, or the Chancery Court of the county palatine of

APPENDIX FIVE: THE PARTNERSHIP ACT 1890

Lancaster, or a county court, may, on the application by summons of any judgment creditor of a partner, make an order charging that partner's interest in the partnership property and profits with payment of the amount of the judgment debt and interest thereon, and may by the same or a subsequent order appoint a receiver of that partner's share of profits (whether already declared or accruing), and of any other money which may be coming to him in respect of the partnership, and direct all accounts and inquiries, and give all other orders and directions which might have been directed or given if the charge had been made in favour of the judgment creditor by the partner, or which the circumstances of the case may require.

(3) The other partner or partners shall be at liberty at any time to redeem the interest charged, or in case of a sale being directed, to purchase the same.

(4) This section shall apply in the case of a cost-book company as if the company were a partnership within the meaning of this Act.

(5) This section shall not apply to Scotland.

24. The interests of partners in the partnership property and their rights and duties in relation to the partnership shall be determined, subject to any agreement express or implied between the partners, by the following rules:

Rules as to interests and duties of partners subject to special agreement.

(1) All the partners are entitled to share equally in the capital and profits of the business, and must contribute equally towards the losses whether of capital or otherwise sustained by the firm.

(2) The firm must indemnify every partner in respect of payments made and personal liabilities incurred by him-

(a) In the ordinary and proper conduct of the business of the firm; or,

(b) In or about anything necessarily done for the preservation of the business or property of the firm.

(3) A partner making, for the purpose of the partnership, any actual payment or advance beyond the amount of capital which he has agreed to subscribe, is entitled to interest at the rate of five per cent, per annum from the date of the payment or advance.

(4) A partner is not entitled, before the ascertainment of profits, to interest on the capital subscribed by him.

(5) Every partner may take part in the management of the partnership business.

(6) No partner shall be entitled to remuneration for acting in the partnership business.

(7) No person may be introduced as a partner without the consent of all existing partners.

(8) Any difference arising as to ordinary matters connected with the partnership business may be decided by a majority of the partners, but no change may be made in the nature of the partnership business without the consent of all existing partners.

(9) The partnership books are to be kept at the place of business of the partnership (or the principal place, if there is more than one), and every partner may, when he thinks fit, have access to and inspect and copy any of them.

Expulsion of partner. **25.** No majority of the partners can expel any partner unless a power to do so has been conferred by express agreement between the partners.

Retirement from partnership at will. **26.**–(1) Where no fixed term has been agreed upon for the duration of the partnership, any partner may determine the partnership at any time on giving notice of his intention so to do to all the other partners.

(2) Where the partnership has originally been constituted by deed, a notice in writing, signed by the partner giving it, shall be sufficient for this purpose.

27.–(1) Where a partnership entered into for a fixed term is continued after the term has expired, and without any express new agreement, the rights and duties of the partners remain the same as they were at the expiration of the term, so far as is consistent with the incidents of a partnership at will. *Where partnership for term is continued over, continuance on old terms presumed.*

(2) A continuance of the business by the partners or such of them as habitually acted therein during the term, without any settlement or liquidation of the partnership affairs, is presumed to be a continuance of the partnership.

28. Partners are bound to render true accounts and full information of all things affecting the partnership to any partner or his legal representatives. *Duty of partners to render accounts, &c.*

29.–(1) Every partner must account to the firm for any benefit derived by him without the consent of the other partners from any transaction concerning the partnership, or from any use by him of the partnership property name or business connexion. *Accountability of partners for private profits.*

(2) This section applies also to transactions undertaken after a partnership has been dissolved by the death of a partner, and before the affairs thereof have been completely wound up, either by any surviving partner or by the representatives of the deceased partner.

30. If a partner, without the consent of the other partners, carries on any business of the same nature as and competing with that of the firm, he must account for and pay over to the firm all profits made by him in that business. *Duty of partner not to compete with firm.*

Rights of assignee of share in partnership

31.–(1) An assignment by any partner of his share in the partnership, either absolute or by way of mortgage or redeemable charge, does not, as against the other partners, entitle the assignee, during the continuance of the partnership, to interfere in the management or administration of the partnership business or affairs, or to require any accounts of the partnership transactions, or to inspect the partnership books, but entitles the assignee only to receive the share of profits to which the assigning partner would otherwise be entitled, and the assignee must accept the account of profits agreed to by the partners.

    (2) In case of a dissolution of the partnership, whether as respects all the partners or as respects the assigning partner, the assignee is entitled to receive the share of the partnership assets to which the assigning partner is entitled as between himself and the other partners, and, for the purpose of ascertaining that share, to an account as from the date of the dissolution.

Dissolution of Partnership, and its consequences.

Dissolution by expiration or notice.

32. Subject to any agreement between the partners a partnership is dissolved-
    (*a*) If entered into for a fixed term, by the expiration of that term:
    (*b*) If entered into for a single adventure or undertaking, by the termination of that adventure or undertaking:
    (*c*) If entered into for an undefined time, by any partner giving notice to the other or others of his intention to dissolve the partnership.

In the last-mentioned case the partnership is dissolved as from the date mentioned in the notice as the date of dissolution, or, if no date is so mentioned, as from the date of the communication of the notice.

APPENDIX FIVE: THE PARTNERSHIP ACT 1890

33.-(1) Subject to any agreement between the partners, every partnership is dissolved as regards all the partners by the death or bankruptcy of any partner. *Dissolution by bankruptcy, death, or charge.*

(2) A partnership may, at the option of the other partners, be dissolved if any partner suffers his share of the partnership property to be charged under this Act for his separate debt.

34. A partnership is in every case dissolved by the happening of any event which makes it unlawful for the business of the firm to be carried on or for the members of the firm to carry it on in partnership. *Dissolution by illegality of partnership.*

35. On application by a partner the Court may decree a dissolution of the partnership in any of the following cases: *Dissolution by the Court.*

(*a*) When a partner is found lunatic by inquisition, or in Scotland by cognition, or is shown to the satisfaction of the Court to be of permanently unsound mind, in either of which cases the application may be made as well on behalf of that partner by his committee or next friend or person having title to intervene as by any other partner:

(*b*) When a partner, other than the partner suing, becomes in any other way permanently incapable of performing his part of the partnership contract:

(*c*) When a partner, other than the partner suing, has been guilty of such conduct as, in the opinion of the Court, regard being had to the nature of the business, is calculated to prejudicially affect the carrying on of the business:

(*d*) When a partner, other than the partner suing, wilfully or persistently commits a breach of the partnership agreement, or otherwise so conducts himself in matters relating to the partnership business that it is not reasonably practicable for the other partner or partners to carry on the business in partnership with him:

(e) When the business of the partnership can only be carried on at a loss:

(f) Whenever in any case circumstances have arisen which, in the opinion of the Court, render it just and equitable that the partnership be dissolved.

Rights of persons dealing with firm against apparent members of firm.

36.—(1) When a person deals with a firm after a change in its constitution he is entitled to treat all apparent members of the old firm as still being members of the firm until he has notice of the change.

(2) An advertisement in the London Gazette as to a firm whose principal place of business is in England or Wales, in the Edinburgh Gazette as to a firm whose principal place of business is in Scotland, and in the Dublin Gazette as to a firm whose principal place of business is in Ireland, shall be notice as to persons who had not dealings with the firm before the date of the dissolution or change so advertised.

(3) The estate of a partner who dies, or who becomes bankrupt, or of a partner who, not having been known to the person dealing with the firm to be a partner, retires from the firm, is not liable for partnership debts contracted after the date of the death, bankruptcy, or retirement respectively.

Right of partners to notify dissolution.

37. On the dissolution of a partnership or retirement of a partner any partner may publicly notify the same, and may require the other partner or partners to concur for that purpose in all necessary or proper acts, if any, which cannot be done without his or their concurrence.

Continuing authority of partners for purposes of winding up.

38. After the dissolution of a partnership the authority of each partner to bind the firm, and the other rights and obligations of the partners, continue

APPENDIX FIVE: THE PARTNERSHIP ACT 1890

notwithstanding the dissolution so far as may be necessary to wind up the affairs of the partnership, and to complete transactions begun but unfinished at the time of the dissolution, but not otherwise.

Provided that the firm is in no case bound by the acts of a partner who has become bankrupt; but this proviso does not affect the liability of any person who has after the bankruptcy represented himself or knowingly suffered himself to be represented as a partner of the bankrupt.

39. On the dissolution of a partnership every partner is entitled, as against the other partners in the firm, and all persons claiming through them in respect of their interests as partners, to have the property of the partnership applied in payment of the debts and liabilities of the firm, and to have the surplus assets after such payment applied in payment of what may be due to the partners respectively after deducting what may be due from them as partners to the firm; and for that purpose any partner or his representatives may on the termination of the partnership apply to the Court to wind up the business and affairs of the firm. *Rights of partners as to application of partnership property.*

40. Where one partner has paid a premium to another on entering into a partnership for a fixed term, and the partnership is dissolved before the expiration of that term otherwise than by the death of a partner, the Court may order the repayment of the premium, or of such part thereof as it thinks just, having regard to the terms of the partnership contract and to the length of time during which the partnership has continued; unless *Apportionment of premium where partnership prematurely dissolved.*

- (*a*) the dissolution is, in the judgment of the Court, wholly or chiefly due to the misconduct of the partner who paid the premium, or
- (*b*) the partnership has been dissolved by an agreement containing no provision for a return of any part of the premium.

THE VALUATION OF BUSINESSES AND SHARES

Rights where partnership dissolved for fraud or misrepresentation.

41. Where a partnership contract is rescinded on the ground of the fraud or misrepresentation of one of the parties thereto, the party entitled to rescind is, without prejudice to any other right, entitled -

(*a*) to a lien on, or right of retention of, the surplus of the partnership assets, after satisfying the partnership liabilities, for any sum of money paid by him for the purchase of a share in the partnership and for any capital contributed by him, and is

(*b*) to stand in the place of the creditors of the firm for any payments made by him in respect of the partnership liabilities, and

(*c*) to be indemnified by the person guilty of the fraud or making the representation against all the debts and liabilities of the firm.

Right of outgoing partner in certain cases to share profits made after dissolution.

42.–(l) Where any member of a firm has died or otherwise ceased to be a partner, and the surviving or continuing partners carry on the business of the firm with its capital or assets without any final settlement of accounts as between the firm and the outgoing partner or his estate, then, in the absence of any agreement to the contrary, the outgoing partner or his estate is entitled at the option of himself or his representatives to such share of the profits made since the dissolution as the Court may find to be attributable to the use of his share of the partnership assets, or to interest at the rate of five per cent, per annum on the amount of his share of the partnership assets.

(2) Provided that where by the partnership contract an option is given to surviving or continuing partners to purchase the interest of a deceased or outgoing partner, and that option is duly exercised, the estate of the deceased partner, or the outgoing partner or his estate, as the case may be, is not entitled to any further or other share of profits; but if any partner assuming to act in exercise of the option does not in all

material respects comply with the terms thereof, he is liable to account under the foregoing provisions of this section.

43. Subject to any agreement between the partners, the amount due from surviving or continuing partners to an outgoing partner or the representatives of a deceased partner in respect of the outgoing or deceased partner's share is a debt accruing at the date of the dissolution or death. Retired or deceased partner's share to be a debt.

44. In settling accounts between the partners after a dissolution of partnership, the following rules shall, subject to any agreement, be observed: Rule for distribution of assets on final settlement of accounts.

(*a*) Losses, including losses and deficiencies of capital, shall be paid firstly out of profits, next out of capital, and lastly, if necessary, by the partners individually in the proportion in which they were entitled to share profits:

(*b*) The assets of the firm including the sums, if any, contributed by the partners to make up losses or deficiencies of capital, shall be applied in the following manner and order:

    1. In paying the debts and liabilities of the firm to persons who are not partners therein:

    2. In paying to each partner rateably what is due from the firm to him for advances as distinguished from capital:

    3. In paying to each partner rateably what is due from the firm to him in respect of capital:

    4. The ultimate residue, if any, shall be divided among the partners in the proportion in which the profits are divisible.

Supplemental.

45. In this Act, unless the contrary intention appears- Definitions of "court" and "business."

The expression "court" includes every court and judge having jurisdiction in the case:

THE VALUATION OF BUSINESSES AND SHARES

The expression "business" includes every trade, occupation, or profession.

<small>Saving for rules of equity and common law.</small>

46. The rules of equity and of common law applicable to partnership shall continue in force except so far as they are inconsistent with the express provisions of this Act.

<small>Provision as to bankruptcy in Scotland.</small>

47.–(1) In the application of this Act to Scotland the bankruptcy of a firm or of an individual shall mean sequestration under the Bankruptcy (Scotland) Acts, and also in the case of an individual the issue against him of a decree of cessio bonorum.

(2) Nothing in this Act shall alter the rules of the law of Scotland relating to the bankruptcy of a firm or of the individual partners thereof.

<small>Repeal.</small>

48. The Acts mentioned in the schedule to this Act are hereby repealed to the extent mentioned in the third column of that schedule.

<small>Commencement of Act.</small>

49. This Act shall come into operation on the first day of January one thousand eight hundred and ninety-one.

<small>Short title.</small>

50. This Act may be cited as the Partnership Act, 1890.

SCHEDULE.

Section 48. ENACTMENTS REPEALED.

Session and Chapter.	Title or Short Title.	Extent of Repeal.
19 & 20 Vict. c. 60.	The Mercantile Law Amendment (Scotland) Act, 1856.	Section seven.
19 & 20 Vict. c. 97.	The Mercantile Law Amendment Act, 1856.	Section four.
28 & 29 Vict. c. 86.	An Act to amend the law of partnership.	The whole Act.

Appendix Six
Tables of Present Value

THE VALUATION OF BUSINESSES AND SHARES

Percentage

Year	1	2	3	4	5	6	7	8	9	10
1	0.990099	0.980392	0.970874	0.961538	0.952381	0.943396	0.934579	0.925926	0.917431	0.909091
2	0.980296	0.961169	0.942596	0.924556	0.907029	0.889996	0.873439	0.857339	0.841680	0.826446
3	0.970590	0.942322	0.915142	0.888996	0.863838	0.839619	0.816298	0.793832	0.772183	0.751315
4	0.960980	0.923845	0.888487	0.854804	0.822702	0.792094	0.762895	0.735030	0.708425	0.683013
5	0.951466	0.905731	0.862609	0.821927	0.783526	0.747258	0.712986	0.680583	0.649931	0.620921
6	0.942045	0.887971	0.837484	0.790315	0.746215	0.704961	0.666342	0.630170	0.596267	0.564474
7	0.932718	0.870560	0.813092	0.759918	0.710681	0.665057	0.622750	0.583490	0.547034	0.513158
8	0.923483	0.853490	0.789409	0.730690	0.676839	0.627412	0.582009	0.540269	0.501866	0.466507
9	0.914340	0.836755	0.766417	0.702587	0.644609	0.591898	0.543934	0.500249	0.460428	0.424098
10	0.905287	0.820348	0.744094	0.675564	0.613913	0.558395	0.508349	0.463193	0.422411	0.385543
11	0.896324	0.804263	0.722421	0.649581	0.584679	0.526788	0.475093	0.428883	0.387533	0.350494
12	0.887449	0.788493	0.701380	0.624597	0.556837	0.496969	0.444012	0.397114	0.355535	0.318631
13	0.878663	0.773033	0.680951	0.600574	0.530321	0.468839	0.414964	0.367698	0.326179	0.289664
14	0.869963	0.757875	0.661118	0.577475	0.505068	0.442301	0.387817	0.340461	0.299246	0.263331
15	0.861349	0.743015	0.641862	0.555265	0.481017	0.417265	0.362446	0.315242	0.274538	0.239392
16	0.852821	0.728446	0.623167	0.533908	0.458112	0.393646	0.338735	0.291890	0.251870	0.217629
17	0.844377	0.714163	0.605016	0.513373	0.436297	0.371364	0.316574	0.270269	0.231073	0.197845
18	0.836017	0.700159	0.587395	0.493628	0.415521	0.350344	0.295864	0.250249	0.211994	0.179859
19	0.827740	0.686431	0.570286	0.474642	0.395734	0.330513	0.276508	0.231712	0.194490	0.163508
20	0.819544	0.672971	0.553676	0.456387	0.376889	0.311805	0.258419	0.214548	0.178431	0.148644

Percentage

Year	11	12	13	14	15	16	17	18	19	20
1	0.900901	0.892857	0.884956	0.877193	0.869565	0.862069	0.854701	0.847458	0.840336	0.833333
2	0.811622	0.797194	0.783147	0.769463	0.756144	0.743163	0.730514	0.718184	0.706165	0.694444
3	0.731191	0.711780	0.693050	0.674972	0.657516	0.640658	0.624371	0.608631	0.593416	0.578704
4	0.658731	0.635518	0.613319	0.592080	0.571753	0.552291	0.533650	0.515789	0.498669	0.482253
5	0.593451	0.567427	0.542760	0.519369	0.497177	0.476113	0.456111	0.437109	0.419049	0.401878
6	0.534641	0.506631	0.480319	0.455587	0.432328	0.410442	0.389839	0.370432	0.352142	0.334898
7	0.481658	0.452349	0.425061	0.399637	0.375937	0.353830	0.333195	0.313925	0.295918	0.279082
8	0.433926	0.403883	0.376160	0.350559	0.326902	0.305025	0.284782	0.266038	0.248671	0.232568
9	0.390925	0.360610	0.332885	0.307508	0.284262	0.262953	0.243404	0.225456	0.208967	0.193807
10	0.352184	0.321973	0.294588	0.269744	0.247185	0.226684	0.208037	0.191064	0.175602	0.161506
11	0.317283	0.287476	0.260698	0.236617	0.214943	0.195417	0.177810	0.161919	0.147565	0.134588
12	0.285841	0.256675	0.230706	0.207559	0.186907	0.168463	0.151974	0.137220	0.124004	0.112157
13	0.257514	0.229174	0.204165	0.182069	0.162528	0.145227	0.129892	0.116288	0.104205	0.093464
14	0.231995	0.204620	0.180677	0.159710	0.141329	0.125195	0.111019	0.098549	0.087567	0.077887
15	0.209004	0.182696	0.159891	0.140096	0.122894	0.107927	0.094888	0.083516	0.073586	0.064905
16	0.188292	0.163122	0.141496	0.122892	0.106865	0.093041	0.081101	0.070776	0.061837	0.054088
17	0.169633	0.145644	0.125218	0.107800	0.092926	0.080207	0.069317	0.059980	0.051964	0.045073
18	0.152822	0.130040	0.110812	0.094561	0.080805	0.069144	0.059245	0.050830	0.043667	0.037561
19	0.137678	0.116107	0.098064	0.082948	0.070265	0.059607	0.050637	0.043077	0.036695	0.031301
20	0.124034	0.103667	0.086782	0.072762	0.061100	0.051385	0.043280	0.036506	0.030836	0.026084

APPENDIX SIX: TABLES OF PRESENT VALUE

Percentage

Year	21	22	23	24	25	26	27	28	29	30
1	0·826446	0·819672	0·813008	0·806452	0·800000	0·793651	0·787402	0·781250	0·775194	0·769231
2	0·683013	0·671862	0·660982	0·650364	0·640000	0·629882	0·620001	0·610352	0·600925	0·591716
3	0·564474	0·550707	0·537384	0·524487	0·512000	0·499906	0·488190	0·476837	0·465834	0·455166
4	0·466507	0·451399	0·436897	0·422974	0·409600	0·396751	0·384402	0·372529	0·361111	0·350128
5	0·385543	0·369999	0·355201	0·341108	0·327680	0·314882	0·302678	0·291038	0·279931	0·269329
6	0·318631	0·303278	0·288781	0·275087	0·262144	0·249906	0·238329	0·227374	0·217001	0·207176
7	0·263331	0·248589	0·234782	0·221844	0·209715	0·198338	0·187661	0·177636	0·168218	0·159366
8	0·217629	0·203761	0·190879	0·178907	0·167772	0·157411	0·147765	0·138778	0·130401	0·122589
9	0·179859	0·167017	0·155187	0·144280	0·134213	0·124930	0·116350	0·108420	0·101086	0·094300
10	0·148644	0·136899	0·126168	0·116354	0·107374	0·099150	0·091614	0·084703	0·078362	0·072538
11	0·122846	0·112213	0·102576	0·093834	0·085899	0·078691	0·072137	0·066174	0·060745	0·055799
12	0·101526	0·091978	0·083395	0·075673	0·068719	0·062453	0·056801	0·051699	0·047089	0·042922
13	0·083905	0·075391	0·067801	0·061026	0·054976	0·049566	0·044725	0·040390	0·036503	0·033017
14	0·069343	0·061796	0·055122	0·049215	0·043960	0·039338	0·035217	0·031554	0·028297	0·025398
15	0·057309	0·050653	0·044815	0·039689	0·035184	0·031221	0·027730	0·024652	0·021936	0·019537
16	0·047362	0·041519	0·036435	0·032008	0·028147	0·024778	0·021834	0·019259	0·017005	0·015028
17	0·039143	0·034032	0·029622	0·025813	0·022518	0·019665	0·017192	0·015046	0·013182	0·011560
18	0·032349	0·027895	0·024083	0·020817	0·018014	0·015607	0·013537	0·011755	0·010218	0·008892
19	0·026735	0·022865	0·019580	0·016788	0·014412	0·012387	0·010659	0·009184	0·007921	0·006840
20	0·022095	0·018741	0·015918	0·013538	0·011529	0·009831	0·008393	0·007175	0·006141	0·005262

Percentage

Year	31	32	33	34	35	36	37	38	35	40
1	0·763359	0·757576	0·751880	0·746269	0·740741	0·735294	0·729927	0·724638	0·719424	0·714286
2	0·582717	0·573921	0·565323	0·556917	0·548697	0·540657	0·532793	0·525100	0·517572	0·510204
3	0·444822	0·434789	0·425055	0·415610	0·406442	0·397542	0·388900	0·380507	0·372354	0·364431
4	0·339559	0·329385	0·319590	0·310156	0·301068	0·292310	0·283869	0·275730	0·267880	0·260308
5	0·259205	0·249534	0·240293	0·231460	0·223014	0·214934	0·207204	0·199804	0·192720	0·185934
6	0·197866	0·189041	0·180672	0·172731	0·165195	0·158040	0·151243	0·144786	0·138647	0·132810
7	0·151043	0·143213	0·135843	0·128904	0·122367	0·116206	0·110397	0·104917	0·099746	0·094865
8	0·115300	0·108495	0·102138	0·096197	0·090642	0·085445	0·080582	0·076027	0·071760	0·067760
9	0·088015	0·082193	0·076795	0·071789	0·067142	0·062828	0·058819	0·055092	0·051626	0·048400
10	0·067187	0·062267	0·057741	0·053574	0·049735	0·046197	0·042933	0·039922	0·037141	0·034572
11	0·051288	0·047172	0·043414	0·039980	0·036841	0·033968	0·031338	0·028929	0·026720	0·024694
12	0·039151	0·035737	0·032642	0·029836	0·027289	0·024977	0·022875	0·020963	0·019223	0·017639
13	0·029886	0·027073	0·024543	0·022266	0·020214	0·018365	0·016697	0·015190	0·013830	0·012599
14	0·022814	0·020510	0·018453	0·016616	0·014974	0·013504	0·012187	0·011008	0·009949	0·008999
15	0·017415	0·015538	0·013875	0·012400	0·011092	0·009929	0·008896	0·007977	0·007158	0·006428
16	0·013294	0·011771	0·010432	0·009254	0·008216	0·007301	0·006493	0·005780	0·005149	0·004591
17	0·010148	0·008918	0·007844	0·006906	0·006086	0·005368	0·004740	0·004188	0·003705	0·003280
18	0·007747	0·006756	0·005898	0·005154	0·004508	0·003947	0·003460	0·003035	0·002665	0·002343
19	0·005914	0·005118	0·004434	0·003846	0·003339	0·002902	0·002525	0·002199	0·001917	0·001673
20	0·004514	0·003877	0·003334	0·002870	0·002474	0·002134	0·001843	0·001594	0·001379	0·001195
21	0·003446	0·002937	0·002507	0·002142	0·001832	0·001569	0·001345	0·001155	0·000992	0·000854
22	0·002630	0·002225	0·001885	0·001598	0·001357	0·001154	0·000962	0·000837	0·000714	0·000610
23	0·002008	0·001686	0·001417	0·001193	0·001005	0·000848	0·000717	0·000606	0·000514	0·000436

Percentage

Year	41	42	43	44	45	46	47	48	49	50
1	0·709220	0·704225	0·699301	0·694444	0·689655	0·684932	0·680272	0·675676	0·671141	0·666667
2	0·502993	0·495933	0·489021	0·432253	0·475624	0·469131	0·462770	0·456538	0·450430	0·444444
3	0·356732	0·349249	0·341973	0·334898	0·328017	0·321323	0·314810	0·308471	0·302302	0·296296
4	0·253002	0·245950	0·239142	0·232568	0·226218	0·220084	0·214156	0·208427	0·202887	0·197531
5	0·179434	0·173204	0·167232	0·161506	0·156013	0·150743	0·145684	0·140829	0·136166	0·131687
6	0·127258	0·121975	0·116946	0·112157	0·107595	0·103248	0·099105	0·095155	0·091387	0·087791
7	0·090254	0·085898	0·081780	0·077887	0·074203	0·070718	0·067418	0·064294	0·061333	0·058528
8	0·064010	0·060491	0·057189	0·054088	0·051175	0·048437	0·045863	0·043442	0·041163	0·039018
9	0·045397	0·042600	0·039992	0·037561	0·035293	0·033176	0·031199	0·029352	0·027626	0·026012
10	0·032197	0·030000	0·027967	0·026084	0·024340	0·022723	0·021224	0·019833	0·018541	0·017342
11	0·022834	0·021127	0·019557	0·018114	0·016786	0·015564	0·014438	0·013401	0·012444	0·011561
12	0·016195	0·014878	0·013676	0·012579	0·011577	0·010660	0·009822	0·009054	0·008352	0·007707
13	0·011486	0·010477	0·009564	0·008735	0·007984	0·007302	0·006682	0·006118	0·005605	0·005138
14	0·008146	0·007378	0·006688	0·006066	0·005506	0·005001	0·004545	0·004134	0·003762	0·003425
15	0·005777	0·005196	0·004677	0·004213	0·003797	0·003425	0·003092	0·002793	0·002525	0·002284
16	0·004097	0·003659	0·003271	0·002926	0·002619	0·002346	0·002103	0·001887	0·001694	0·001522
17	0·002906	0·002577	0·002287	0·002032	0·001806	0·001607	0·001431	0·001275	0·001137	0·001015
18	0·002061	0·001815	0·001599	0·001411	0·001246	0·001101	0·000973	0·000862	0·000763	0·000677
19	0·001462	0·001278	0·001118	0·000980	0·000859	0·000754	0·000662	0·000582	0·000512	0·000451
20	0·001037	0·000900	0·000782	0·000680	0·000592	0·000516	0·000450	0·000393	0·000344	0·000301

INDEX

'Angry' valuation. *see* valuation
AOL, **1**-23
Articles of Association, **2**-14
Assets, **2**-37—**2**-38, Chapter **6**

Bad investment, **11**-13
BDO Stoy Hayward Private Company Price Index (PCPI), **4**-13, **4**-15
 "Private Equity Price Index", **4**-14
Benign Valuation, **1**-02
Bowes, David
 Tolley's Practical Share and Business Evaluation, **2**-43
Buying and Selling a Business: Tax and Legal Issues. see Irish Taxation Institute

Capital Acquisitions Tax, **4**-16, **4**-17, **7**-10
Cases referred to
 Colgan v. Coglan & Colgan (1993), **11**-13
 Dean v. Prince (1954), **14**-02, **14**-05
 Ebrahimi v. Westbourne Galleries Ltd (1972), **11**-08
 Holt v. IRC (1953), **4**-03
 IRC v. Muller (1901), **6**-27
 Jones v. Sherwood Computer Services Ltd (2002), **1**-03
 Larkin v. Phoenix Office Supplies Ltd (2002), **11**-11
 Loveday v. Renton (1990), **App.** 2
Commercial Due Diligence: The Key to Understanding Value in an Acquisition. see Howson, Peter
Company Law. see Keane, Ronan
Company law and valuations, **2**-12—**2**-15, **2**-21—**2**-24
Compulsory Acquisition, **2**-22
Courtney, Thomas B.
 The Law of Private Companies, **1**-17, **2**-14
Cremins, Denis
 "Valuation of Shares", **14**-08

Deadlock provision, **13**-08—**13**-10
 Desk Valuation, **2**-40
Discounted Cash Flows (DCF), **2**-46, **3**-02—**3**-03, Chapter **10**
 Divided Valuation, **2**-31, **3**-12, **5**-03—**5**-12, **6**-13

Due diligence, **2**–45, **2**–50, **3**–15
Due Diligence: A Practical Guide. see Williams, Vanessa
 Duty of Core, **1**–06

Easy entry, **2**–45
EBITDA, **2**–46, **4**–22
Embarrassment Clause, **5**–14
Errors, Common, **2**–05, **2**–06
Expert, acting as, **1**–07, **1**–14

Fair Value, Chapter **14**
Fees, for valuation, **1**–08, **1**–09, **1**–18, ***App.*** Two
Financial Times sector indices, **4**–11
 Forecasts, business, **3**–06
Formula purchases, **7**–06, **7**–08
Future maintainable profits, **2**–31, **2**–32, Chapter **3**

Glover, Christopher
 Valuation of Unquoted Companies, The **2**–44
Goodwill, **6**–21 — **6**–30, **17**–07, **17**–21 — **17**–25

Hindsight, **4**–03, **4**–04
Howson, Peter
 Commercial Due Diligence: The Key to Understanding Value in an Acquisition, **3**–15

Indicative Valuation, **2**–39, **2**–40
Investment companies, **2**–46, **5**–02, **6**–02, **6**–10, **6**–12,
 6–16 — **6**–18, **14**–03
Intellectual property, Chapter **16**
Irish Taxation Institute
 Buying and Selling a Business: Tax and Legal Issues, **3**–15

Keane, Ronan
 Company Law, **2**–14

Law of Private Companies, The. see Courtney, Thomas B.
Letter of Confidentiality, **8**–09
Letter of Confirmation from Directors, **1**–10, **3**–03, ***App.*** One
Letter of Engagement, **1**–08, **1**–09, **2**–50, ***App.*** Two
 a. non-contested circumstances
 b. contested circumstances
 c. desktop valuation
'*Lifestyle*' businesses, **8**–01

INDEX

Majority Shareholding, **2**–12, **2**–13, **2**–21, **2**–23, **2**–29, **2**–31
Management accounts, **3**–14
Management buyout (MBO), Chapter **15**
Marital separation, **1**–01, **1**–11, **8**–01
Market sentiment, **4**–05 — **4**–07
Market value, **8**–08, Chapter **14**
Minority discount, **5**–02, **5**–13
Minority shareholding, **1**–17, **2**–19 — **2**–24, **2**–29, **2**–31, **2**–34, Chapter **5**
Multiple of profits, Chapter **4**

Net assets. *see* assets
'Net present value' (NPV), **10**–02, **10**–3, **10**–09, **10**–12

Open market value. *see* market value
'Oppression of minority', **1**–17, **2**–20, **6**–18, **11**–01

Partnership Act 1890, **17**–07, *App.* 5
Partnership agreement, **17**–18 — **17**–20
Partnership Law. see Twomey, Michael
   Present Value Tables, *App.* Six
Preset Value Tables, *App.* Six
Price/earning ratio (P/E), **2**–02, **4**–02, **4**–05 — **4**–15
Pricing power, **2**–45, **3**–16 — **3**–18, **16**-07
Professional practices, Chapter **17**
Purchaser of business, **3**–07
   care required, **3**–08

Quasi-partnership, **14**–03, Chapter **11**

'Ransom' shareholding, **2**–35
Reasoned valuation, **1**–03 — **1**–04
Revenue valuations, **4**–16, *App.* Four
   on share valuation, **4**–17
'Rules of thumb', **2**–06, **2**–33, Chapter **7**

Shareholders' Agreement, **1**–13, **2**–17, **2**–18, Chapter **13**
Special purchaser, Chapter **12**
Special Resolution, **2**–13

Tax Law/Cases and Valuation, **14**–09
Tolley's Practical Share and Business Evaluation. see Bowes, David
Twomey, Michael
   Partnership Law, **17**–08

Valuation Reports, *App.* Three
   a. *contested circumstances*
   b. *desktop valuation*
   c. *straightforward valuation*
Valuing small businesses, Chapter **9**
Valuation of Unquoted Companies, The. see Glover, Christopher

Williams, Vanessa
   Due Diligence: A Practical Guide, **3**–15
Willing seller/willing buyer, **14**–10
   concept of, **14**–09
Working papers, **2**–50